THE DRUG CRISIS
AND THE CHURCH

BOOKS BY HENLEE H. BARNETTE

Published by The Westminster Press

The Drug Crisis and the Church
Crucial Problems in Christian Perspective
The New Theology and Morality

THE DRUG CRISIS
AND
THE CHURCH

by
HENLEE H. BARNETTE

THE WESTMINSTER PRESS
Philadelphia

ISBN 0–664–24921–3

LIBRARY OF CONGRESS CATALOG CARD No. 73–148563

BOOK DESIGN BY
DOROTHY ALDEN SMITH

Published by The Westminster Press ®
Philadelphia, Pennsylvania

PRINTED IN THE UNITED STATES OF AMERICA

To
Wayne Edward Oates

Comrade and Counselor
"in season and out of season"

CONTENTS

PREFACE

OF THE WRITING of books on drugs, their use and abuse, there is no end. So why another one? The reasons: (1) there is a paucity of works that include the role of the church in ministering to people behind the chemical curtain; (2) the church generally manifests an attitude of disdain toward drug users and addicts and therefore expresses little concern and concrete action for their redemption; and (3) some ministers tend to become peddlers of panic when they discuss the problem from the pulpit and in print.

It is the purpose of this volume to present as objectively and accurately as possible an overview of the drug problem in terms of the nature, etiology, and effects of drugs, along with some suggestions for the rehabilitation of the drug dependent.

To flesh out this purpose, Chapter 1 describes our drug-oriented society. Chapter 2 is concerned with the identification of some of the most commonly abused drugs. In Chapter 3 there is a discussion of the causative factors in drug abuse. Chapter 4 is devoted to ways of coping with the drug issue in terms of legal action. Parents who confront the problem of drug abuse among their progeny are provided with some guidelines in Chapter 5. Therapies for drug abusers are described in Chapter 6. Chapters 7 through 10 deal with the religious dimensions of the drug problem. A selected bibliography along with appendixes containing suggested film resources, a glossary of drug jargon, and a list of the regional offices of the Bureau of Narcotics and Dangerous Drugs, where information may be obtained about drug abuse, appears at the end of the volume.

Immediately the question arises as to whether or not anyone who has never smoked pot, "dropped" LSD, "sniffed" heroin, and "shot speed" can understand the drug problem or speak with any authority about it. Can one who has never had the "experience" tell others about the effects and dangers of drugs? As a college student warned when he learned that the writer was doing this study: "If you haven't tried it, don't knock it." Richard Alpert, formerly a professor at Harvard University and an advocate of the use of LSD, thinks that a person cannot adequately discuss the effects of drugs, particularly psychedelics, unless he has tried them. He concedes, however, that some experiences such as "profound love," "moments of great tragedy," and "sexual orgasm" do provide one with some experiential frame of reference. These are moments of self-transcendence when we "go out of our minds," but they do not provide the same intensity and quality of experience to be derived from certain drugs.[1]

One may ask with Sidney Cohen, whose expertise about drugs is unquestionable, whether those on LSD really understand the issues involved, such as the quality of the "experience," the insight, and the revelation that allegedly come from ingesting the drug, and why they attempt to find joy in a "pot" party.[2] Does one really have to "experience" drugs to understand such issues?

This writer thinks not. Many doctors and specialists who have never ingested dangerous drugs have developed considerable skill in dealing with the physical, psychological, and social effects of drugs. Even a theologian may have some understanding of these issues without "tripping" on drugs.

Admittedly, my own qualifications for writing about drugs are limited. I have never ingested hallucinogenic drugs, nor have I been "strung out" on heroin. My "experience" with drugs is quite innocent, since I have been a user of only caffeine, nicotine, and aspirin—all drugs nevertheless. Oh, yes, I was on an assortment of painkiller pills and capsules, including Darvon, after two surgical operations.

Among the things that I have done which may qualify me to speak about drugs and drug abuse are: as chauffeur for an addict in my younger years, I learned something of the horrors of heroin and its decimating effects upon those hooked on it, and their families; participation in conferences and seminars on narcotics and dangerous drugs; visits to narcotic hospitals and drug information centers; an attempt to teach a course in a seminary, which forced me to examine carefully the literature on drugs and their effects; and, finally, interviews and dialogues with young people on drugs, which placed me in personal relationship with them and helped me to understand their attitudes and actions.

My thanks are due to many persons and agencies for help in preparing this book. Dr. James Graves, librarian at the National Institute of Mental Health Clinical Research Center at Lexington, Kentucky, graciously gave me free use of the Center's library. Other personnel of the Center introduced me to residents in the institution whom I interviewed. John Hollon, director of the Drug Abuse Information and Education Center, Inc., of Louisville, Kentucky, provided me and my students at Southern Baptist Seminary with the opportunity to see first hand how such an agency operates to aid drug abusers. Personnel at the University of Kentucky College of Pharmacy permitted me to use its library facilities.

To Dr. Foy Valentine, Executive Secretary of the Christian Life Commission of the Southern Baptist Convention, I wish to express my appreciation for inviting me to give the lectures on drug abuse at the Commission's Annual Conference at Glorieta, New Mexico. This volume is an expansion of the lectures.

To my wife, Helen, who has been both my best critic and counselor in the preparation of this book, I extend my deepest gratitude. Mrs. Nancy Stiltner and Mrs. Carole Batchelder typed the manuscript, and I thank them for their persistence and patience.

H. H. B.

Louisville, Kentucky

CHAPTER 1

A DRUG-ORIENTED SOCIETY

AMERICANS of all ages are ingesting drugs from nicotine to narcotics, from aspirin to "acid." Thousands are tripping on pills and powders of all kinds. In the mornings, stimulants, or "uppers," are taken to wake up, and in the evenings, sedatives, or "downers," to go to sleep. Such is the Yo-Yo existence of many.

1. PREVALENCE OF THE PROBLEM

Prescription or permissive drugs are available for "anything that ails you." Almost twenty-seven million pounds of aspirin are produced annually in the United States. This is sufficient to take care of seventeen billion headaches! Twelve billion amphetamine and barbiturate tablets and capsules, along with fifty million tranquilizers, are manufactured annually in this nation. About half of these find their way into the illegal market.[1] In a typical year, Americans consume a prescribed one hundred and fifty thousand pounds of amphetamines and nine hundred and seventy-nine thousand pounds of barbiturates.[2] Tons of marijuana pour into this country each year from Mexico and other countries, not to mention that which

is produced covertly. Numerous clandestine factories produce LSD, and the family medicine cabinet is a pot-
pourri of drugs easily available to children and young
people.

No one knows the exact number who abuse drugs, but
reports indicate that the problem has reached epidemic
proportions. Epidemiological studies reveal that drug experimentation and abuse is on the increase among children, youth, and older people of every class.

Once confined to people in the ghetto, drug abuse has
now migrated to the middle and upper classes in suburbia. Recently, the nineteen-year-old son of the governor
of New Jersey was arrested in Philadelphia for possessing
marijuana. The seventeen-year-old son of the contender
for the governorship of New York was arrested in Greenwich Village for possession of hashish and barbiturates.
An eighteen-year-old son of a circuit court judge was arrested on charges of possessing packets of heroin. Now
the mayor of New York City has said that he was not
aware that his children smoked pot (marijuana), but that
he wouldn't be surprised if they had.[3]

Speaking of pot, Dr. Stanley Yolles, formerly director
of the National Institute of Mental Health, puts the
number of Americans who have used it at least once at
twelve million and says that it could be as high as twenty
million.[4] There are no exact statistics on the ingestion
of this drug, but one suspects that it falls somewhere between the two figures provided by Yolles. For years marijuana was largely a problem among the lower classes.
Now it has lost its stigma because the "nice kids," sons
and daughters of professional people, governmental figures, and affluent suburbanites, are experimenting with
it and abusing it.

Because pot parties have migrated to the suburbs, producers of alcoholic beverages are concerned that pot may become a substitute for cocktails and beer. One popular song, "The Six Pack" (beer), calls the pot and LSD users back to beer. Since pot is being used by "respectable" adults and youth, the attitude of the law-and-order people, the opinion-makers, is changing to a more lenient one. But all this understanding and tolerance does not stem from a sense of compassion; rather, it is due to the fact that some of their own children in the best schools have begun to "turn on" with pot. Now they are called "experimenters" or "faddists" instead of the "dope fiends" of the "slums." Even Barry Goldwater, a strong law-and-order exponent, admits that laws against marijuana are too harsh and unenforceable.

Drug experimentation and abuse among college students is mushrooming. This experimentation occurs on every college campus in America. From Harvard to Berkeley, from Florida University to Texas State, no campus is free of drugs. Estimates indicate that from 15 to 50 percent of college students use marijuana and LSD.[5] This, of course, does not include other illicit drugs used by students.

James Carey, in his excellent study of the drug scene in and around Berkeley University, estimates that there are 10,000 to 25,000 illegal drug users in that area.[6] A survey of the student body of the University of Louisville in 1969 revealed that 21 percent of the students had smoked pot as compared to the national average of 22 percent. About 5 percent have used LSD, which is approximately the same as the national sample.[7]

The drug revolution, which began on college campuses a few years ago, has now seeped down into the high schools. According to one report, the use of drugs, particularly marijuana, has become an acceptable fact of life for from 30 to 50 percent of all the U.S. junior and high school students.[8] At Greenwich, Connecticut, a high school newspaper took a sample of homeroom classes and reported that 46 percent of all seniors had smoked marijuana, 10 percent had tried LSD, and 3 percent had used heroin. Similar figures are found in other secondary schools around the nation.[9]

Secondary school students use all kinds of drugs ranging from the fumes of certain types of glue to hard narcotics. Some high school students seeking "kicks" play what is called "fruit salad." After removing all the drugs in the family medicine cabinet, they place the pills in a bowl or on the floor and each member of the group takes one of every pill or capsule. These indiscriminate combinations of drugs can produce "real freak-outs."

Harder drugs, especially heroin, are becoming more prevalent in urban communities. In a house-to-house survey of a forty-block section of New York City's Harlem area, investigators discovered that almost one out of every three persons was addicted to "hard drugs." Eighteen thousand addicts were in this area, of whom 2,000 were children under the age of sixteen. Of these 2,000 children, 1,800, or 90 percent, lived by themselves without the presence of an adult.[10]

Recently in the city of New York, a twelve-year-old boy, Ralph de Jesus, was discovered to be a "junkie," or a user of heroin. After a stint in a hospital where he had been seriously ill with hepatitis, contracted from a dirty needle he used to "mainline" (to inject directly in the vein in the arm) heroin, he was released to the Odyssey House (rehabilitation center) for treatment. Later he was taken to testify before a New York State Legislature Committee investigating addiction among the young. The frightening thing is that Ralph's case is not a special one, for there are thousands of others his age and even younger who are hooked on heroin.[11]

Heroin is a dangerous drug. An overdose (OD) can kill the user. In 1969 more than 900 persons died of heroin use in New York City. Of these, 224 were teen-agers, and 24 of them were under the age of fifteen.[12]

In Louisville, Kentucky, heroin, once confined to central and western sections of the city, is now invading the eastern area. Young heroin users interviewed estimate that there are as many as 200 youths in eastern Louisville and Jefferson County who are users. These are "nice" kids from respectable families.[13] No community, regardless of size, is immune from the threat of hard drugs.

The use of drugs among military men is on the increase. Military doctors report that the use of marijuana by GI's is worsening in Vietnam, where it is as easy to purchase as beer. Army medical officers report that studies show that 30 percent of the soldiers have used pot or other drugs, and that the percentage is rising. Prior to the arrival of American soldiers, little marijuana was grown in Vietnam, but now it is plentiful and of greater strength than that grown in the United States.[14] Dr. Gordon Livingston, a former medical officer, told a conference on War and National Responsibility in Washington, D.C., that the use of drugs among U.S. troops in Vietnam had reached epidemic proportions. He estimated that drug experimentation runs as high as 80 percent, with many GI's becoming addicted.[15]

The military has been slow to recognize drug abuse as an illness. The military needs to recognize it as a sickness and respond with an adequate therapeutic program. Dr. Joel H. Kaplan, army psychiatrist in Vietnam, has proposed that the Army admit it has a drug problem, that it set up a thorough educational program on drugs, that soldiers who abuse drugs be treated as patients with a medical problem, and that the Vietnamese be forced to stop the traffic in marijuana.[16]

As these soldiers return to their homes in the United States, they will bring their drug problems with them to add to the burgeoning drug issue here. Drugs have already become prevalent among soldiers on military bases in this country. Some returning veterans carry heavy psychological burdens from their participation in war and may continue the use of drugs as a means of withdrawal from society.

Arrests on drug charges are on the increase. Marijuana and narcotic arrests have climbed 322 percent over the past ten years and three fourths of those apprehended were under twenty-five. Many of them were from middle- and upper-class families.[17] These figures, of course, provide only a partial picture of the extent of the drug problem. Thousands of drug users are never apprehended by the police. One can only conclude that the iceberg analogy of the drug problem is correct—nine tenths of it is under the surface.

2. Sources of the Drug Supply

Sources of the drug supply are numerous. Some drugs, such as barbiturates and amphetamines, come from the family medicine cabinet. But this is not the major source. Perhaps as much as 50 percent of legitimate pharmaceutical products are diverted into illicit channels and are sold by pushers to the drug culture.

Drugs are sometimes obtained by fraud. An abuser might steal a physician's prescription pad, forge a prescription, take it to the drugstore where the pharmacist unknowingly fills it. Again, the drug abuser may change a legitimate prescription and write in a greater amount of drugs. Some drug dependents have been known to borrow or steal prescriptions from others and have them filled.

Some addicts become "drugstore beaters," who obtain drugs by burglarizing pharmacies. Morphine, Dilaudid, and other opiates are the drugs they crave. A typical drugstore beater is an addict who must have a supply each day which may cost from $100 to $150. If his wife is an addict, the cost will be about $250 per day in black-market drugs. Hence, he is forced to steal enough drugs for each day to avoid the pain of withdrawal sickness. He is almost always a junkie or pusher who sells to friends to help support his own habit.

Every large city has its hangout for drug abusers. Parks are favorite places in many urban communities. Hogan's Fountain in Cherokee Park has been a gathering place for young people on drugs in Louisville, Kentucky. In the spring of 1970, a reporter spent seven nights at Hogan's Fountain and observed sellers on hand to supply drugs. About fifty boys and girls were seen coming and going at the Fountain. On weekend nights the number reached over one hundred. Their ages ranged from about fourteen to the mid-twenties. The reporter observed youths smoking marijuana while swinging in the park's swing sets nearby. He saw drugs change hands and was offered mescaline, amphetamines, LSD, cocaine, hashish, barbiturates, and marijuana at the current price. The police have cracked down on these drug abusers, but they scatter, go underground, and then reappear.[18]

Manufacturers of illegal drugs set up laboratories in garages, basements, and abandoned warehouses. Principally they produce LSD. Three such labs were discovered in Louisville in 1970, one in a garage and two in basements. Amateur chemists operate these labs to supply the growing drug culture. Often drugs are mailed out or picked up by young people, primarily students, who drive in from nearby cities. Most of the marijuana coming into this country arrives from Mexico over a thinly patrolled border. It comes in by plane, brought by tourists and professional smugglers. However, since marijuana grows in most temperate areas, it is found growing wild in many places in the United States. "Kentucky Blue" is a homegrown "grass" (marijuana) and is found on many farms and in uncultivated fields. Young people gather it and prepare it for use.

Some physicians contribute to the drug problem by prescribing too many drugs to their patients. Dr. Donald B. Louria, associate professor of medicine at Cornell University, charges: "At the present time, it is a reasonable estimate that half of the sedatives and tranquilizers prescribed by physicians are given unnecessarily.[19]

Most of the heroin that arrives in the United States comes from opium poppies grown in Turkey, Mexico, and Southeast Asia. But Turkey is the biggest supplier of the drug. American officials estimate that 80 percent of the heroin brought to the United States originates in the Turkish poppy fields. There it is legally grown for the government. Some of the raw opium is held back by the farmers and sold on the black market. It is purchased at three times that of the legal price by criminals who smuggle it into France and other European countries, where it is converted into heroin in secret laboratories. Eventually it is smuggled into this country.

To stop the flow of heroin at its source the United States has provided a three-million-dollar loan to Turkey to control the diversion of the opium crop into the black market. All reports indicate that the program has had little effect in cutting off the illegal heroin supply.

The above are some, but not all, of the sources of the drug supply in this country. More and more people are drawing on these sources of supply. Hence, we are now a drug-dependent society. It is a chemical culture in which we take pills to pep us up and to calm us down, to gain weight and to lose weight, to get a thrill and to escape reality. Most of the abusers of drugs in this nation are white, young, and affluent. But drug usage is not determined by a person's race, religion, national origin, or class. Drug abuse cuts across all segments and strata of our contemporary society.

CHAPTER 2

DRUG IDENTIFICATION

ONE OF THE FIRST STEPS in coping with the drug crisis is to define, identify, and classify drugs that are dangerous. Most of us are without the pharmacological expertise necessary to recognize and discriminate between given drugs, especially in terms of their chemical content. However, it is hoped that this chapter will provide the reader with some knowledge as to the nature of drugs and how they are classified by the pharmacist.

1. DEFINITION OF A DRUG AND DRUG TERMINOLOGY

To provide some precision as to drugs and drug abuse, some definitions are in order. A "drug" has different meanings for people. In the popular sense of the term, a drug is a medicine usually prescribed by a physician, but this tells us nothing about its chemical contents and effects. Thus, the first dictionary definition of "drug" is "any substance used as a medicine or as an ingredient in medicine." [1]

From a pharmacological point of view, a drug is "any substance that by its chemical nature alters structure or function in the living organism." [2] For this study, a sharper concept is necessary. Hence, as an operational definition, a drug is any chemical substance capable of changing the mood and manner of persons who ingest it. The effect of a drug may be harmful or helpful, depending upon the amount and repetition of dosage, the type of drug, specific environmental circumstances, and the physical and psychological condition of the ingester.

"Drug addiction" is also defined in different ways. Richard R. Lingeman says that drug addiction is "an overwhelming involvement with, and craving for, a substance, often accompanied by physical dependence, which motivates continuous usage, resulting in a syndrome of indefinable symptoms appearing when the drug is suddenly withdrawn." [3] Sidney Cohen lists some of the characteristics of addiction: a compulsion to continue taking a drug; a tendency to increase the dosage; a psychic and generally a physical dependence; and harmful effects on the user and society. [4]

The term "drug addiction" is thought by some to be too general and imprecise. For example, the World Health Organization's Expert Committee on Addiction-Producing Drugs has substituted the term "drug dependence," which stresses the fact that characteristics will vary with the person involved. These characteristics must be made clear by indicating the particular type of drug dependence—morphine, amphetamine, hallucinogen, etc.—in each specific case. [5]

"Drug abuse" is a term frequently used by recent writers on the subject of the drug problem. It is defined by Cohen as "the persistent and usually excessive self-administration of any drug which has resulted in psychological or physical dependence." [6]

"Tolerance" is a word that designates the diminishing

effect of a drug and the need for increased dosage to obtain the same experience of the original dose. "Physical dependence" refers to a changed physiological state due to repeated dosage of a drug which requires a continuation of its use to prevent withdrawal sickness. "Psychological dependence" refers to a psychic compulsion that requires continued use of a drug for a feeling of pleasure and satisfaction. "Withdrawal" syndrome or symptoms indicate the condition of illness that occurs when a drug is abruptly withdrawn after a period of use.

2. Drug Types

Drug identification charts, kits, or dial-a-drug devices are produced as educational aids for people who are concerned about drug abuse. But these gadgets can only provide data as to what drugs look like in terms of the shape, size, and color given them by the manufacturers. For the classification of various kinds of drugs, these devices are helpful, but for the identification of their actual chemical content, they provide no information.

Different types of drugs often appear in capsules or pills of the same size and color. Only a chemist can identify the active ingredient contained. Many of these drugs have no identifying monogram. Approximately 75 percent of the illicit drugs on the market have no identification marks. Even those which do can be counterfeited.

Another problem related to the identification of drugs is the enormous number of stimulants and sedatives produced. More than 2,500 types of amphetamines are on the market, and over the past sixty years chemists have synthesized an equal number of barbiturate types of compounds to assist persons in search of relief from tensions, anxieties, and insomnia.[7] In all, about 30,000 preparations of drugs are on the druggists' shelves.

Identification of drugs in the human body can be done only by blood and urine tests. Only by tests can one detect whether a person is on barbiturates or amphetamines. A person may be arrested for drunken driving, but tests will reveal no alcohol content in his blood because he was high on amphetamines, barbiturates, or some other drug.

Chemical identification is essential in detecting types of drugs that come packaged in multitudinous forms and shapes. Hence, children and any young people should be admonished never to take a drug in tablet or capsule form without a doctor's prescription. Recently in Louisville a seventeen-year-old boy was rushed to a hospital after collapsing at one of the high schools. He had taken an amphetamine tablet purchased from a fifteen-year-old boy who had bought it from a stranger in the park.

3. CLASSIFICATION OF DRUGS

Drugs are classified broadly as illicit (prohibited) and legal (permissible), hard and soft, addicting and non-addicting. Since this study is concerned with those drugs most commonly abused in our society, they are classified under five rubrics: stimulants, sedatives, organic solvents, hallucinogens, and narcotics.

a. Stimulants ("Uppers")

About 20 percent of all drugs prescribed by physicians for lifting the mood involve stimulants. Among the most abused amphetamines are Benzedrine, Dexedrene, and

Methedrine. These drugs appear in tablets and capsules. Tablets are round and heart-shaped, and are blue, yellow, and pink in color. They are given such slang names as bennies, footballs, hearts, wake-ups, speed, skyrockets, cartwheels, copilots, diet pills, and pep pills.

Since amphetamines directly stimulate the central nervous system, they are prescribed for the treatment of depression, weight control, and narcolepsy (sleepiness), as well as to promote wakefulness, to combat fatigue, and to increase energy.

Abuse of amphetamines produces excitability, paranoid tendencies, restlessness, irritability, hallucinations, insomnia, dilated pupils, and aggressiveness. Since these drugs increase blood pressure, there is the danger of a heart attack. While their use does not result in physical dependence, psychic dependence may develop.

Amphetamines are legal only by prescription. The Drug Abuse Control Amendment of 1965 brings the manufacture and distribution of amphetamines under federal control. Penalities for violation of the laws relating to drugs will be discussed in Chapter 4.

b. Sedatives ("Downers")

Sedatives are produced for medical purposes to relax the central nervous system. Among the most frequently abused sedatives are the barbiturates. Developed in Germany in 1846, numerous types have been synthesized and prepared for medical use under various trade names. Seconal is supplied in bright-red capsules (hence, the slang names are: red birds, red devils, or reds); Nembutal appears in all-yellow or yellow-white capsules (nembies, nemmies, and yellow jackets); Amytals are blue (blue birds and blue heavens); Tuinals are blue and red (rainbows). Among the other commonly abused barbiturates are phenobarbital, Dexamyl, and Butisol.

Medically, barbiturates are prescribed as depressants, hypnotics, and sedatives for the relief of nervousness, anxiety, and tension. Since they are used to combat insomnia, they are popularly known as sleeping pills.

When abused, barbiturates impair the ability to think clearly and to work. The abuser may stagger, drop objects, or fall into a deep sleep. These drugs are dangerous and may produce physical dependence. Withdrawal symptoms are usually more dangerous than those resulting from narcotics and may include an epileptic type of convulsion, delirium, mental confusion, and hallucinations. An overdose (OD) can result in death due to a depressed respiratory function. Because they are so dangerous, barbiturates are legal only by a doctor's prescription.

c. Organic Solvents ("Sniffers")

Inhaling the fumes from certain organic solvents (volatile hydrocarbons) for a quick "high" occurs among young people from about nine to eighteen years of age. Glue, plastic cement, gasoline, lighter fluid, ether, paint thinner, and aerosols are among the most abused fumes.

Model-airplane glue is probably the most highly abused of the group. The sniffers squeeze the glue onto a piece of cloth or into a bag from which the fumes are inhaled. Gasoline and paint thinner are inhaled directly from the tank or can.

At first the glue sniffer experiences a tingling sensation in the head, a lightness and an exhilaration known to him as a "jag." If he continues to inhale the fumes, he will experience a state similar to alcoholic intoxication, which may last from thirty to forty-five minutes, depending on the amount inhaled. A second stage lasting about an hour usually follows with symptoms of drowsiness, stupor, and sometimes unconsciousness. Some users learn to stay high on glue for long periods of time. Habitual users may use as many as five tubes of airplane glue a day.

Effects resulting from glue sniffing are inflamed eyes, irritated nose and lung tissue, loss of appetite and weight, a feeling of sickness. Habitual users may suffer toxic damage to the liver, kidneys, brain, and the bone marrow. Though physical dependence does not appear to result from glue sniffing, it may lead to detrimental effects on emotional health. It may result in a loss of motivation expressed in irresponsibility, absence from school, or dropping out altogether.

Several states have passed laws regulating glue sniffing. Maryland, for example, makes it a misdemeanor. Some retailers have curbed its access by ceasing to stock airplane glue or questioning habitual buyers of glue, paint thinner, and lighter fluid. A law should be enacted to force the manufacturers to put some repelling ingredient in glue to discourage sniffers.

d. Hallucinogens ("Mind Expanders")

Perhaps the most abused drugs are the hallucinogens or psychedelic (mind-expanding) drugs. Among these are LSD-25, marijuana, mescaline, peyote, and psilocybin. Although there are other drugs in this category, only the most commonly abused can be considered in this study.

(1) *LSD.* One of the most powerful of the hallucinogenic drugs is LSD-25 (*d*-lysergic acid diethylamide tar-

trate 25). It was discovered by Dr. Albert Hofmann, a Swiss biochemist, in 1938, as a result of research with products of fermented rye. In 1943, five years later, Hofmann discovered its psychoactive properties when he accidentally swallowed a bit of it. As a result, he was ushered into a weird realm of odd-shaped objects of vivid colors.

LSD is produced from ergot, a fungus, which grows as a rust on wheat and rye plants. It is a white crystalline powder which is tasteless, odorless, and colorless. As a liquid the drug has a slight bluish or purplish color which can be soaked up into chewing gum, sugar cubes, tablets, animal crackers, or applied to postage stamps for ready use. Slang names for LSD include: acid, pearly gates, cubes, heavenly blue, and wedding bells.

So potent is LSD that a single ounce will produce 300,000 average doses for human beings. An amount smaller than a grain of salt can produce psychotic effects in some people. A mere speck, 1/280,000 of an ounce, has an effect usually from eight to ten hours. Normally it is taken orally, but can be injected into the veins for a quicker high.

As for the physical effects of LSD, it increases the heart pulse and rate, causes a rise in blood pressure and temperature, dilates the pupils of the eyes. Tremors of the hands and feet, cold sweaty palms, a flushed face or paleness, shivering, chills, irregular breathing, nausea, and a loss of appetite are also results produced by this drug.

While LSD is not physically addicting, it does produce profound psychological effects.[8] One hour after ingestion, effects of the drug begin to appear. The initial reaction is that of anxiety and mild nausea. As the drug really takes effect the user's perception of himself in time and space is distorted. Flat objects take on three-dimensional shapes. Walls appear to move. Taste, smell, hearing, and touch seem to be more acute. Sensory impression may be translated or merged into one another. For example, music may appear as colors, and colors may seem to have a taste.

Users of LSD have hallucinations of flowers, animals, and other people, which they perceive to be hallucinations, though powerless to stop them. Barriers between themselves and others appear to come down, and they may have the feeling of merging with the external world. Normal recognition of boundaries between body and space may be lost, which can give users the notion that they can fly freely or float.

Sometimes the user of LSD has an unpleasant "trip" or a "freak-out." Objects, swirling colors, and shapes may become terrifying and threatening. A bad trip may occur after several pleasant ones. A student reported a frightening third trip as follows:

I saw the most horrible, slimy snake I had ever seen. . . . It circled around me, starting at my ankles and slowly winding up my legs. I tried to get free but I couldn't, my legs seemed to become part of the snake. . . . I knew the snake was swallowing me, bit by bit. . . . The snake began to swallow my head. . . . I was the snake without eyelids, so I had to watch everything.[9]

Some who drop LSD claim to have a religious or mystical experience and feel at one with the Absolute. Jeff, a high school student, related to students in a seminary class that on trips he felt at one with nature and that nature was everything, including God, and that since he was a part of nature, he himself was God.

Is LSD dangerous? Reports from hospitals where "acidheads" have been treated warn of definite dangers: panic, paranoia, and recurrence. Days and weeks after some persons stop taking LSD, the thing they saw and felt while on the drug may recur and make them fearful of going insane. Since the LSD user feels that he can fly, he may jump from a high window to his death or he may walk in front of a car because he thinks he cannot be hurt.

Some medical doctors think that LSD can lead to mental illness. Others claim that it may result in chromosomal damage. Studies purport to show chromosomal damage in human leukocytes induced by LSD.[10] Birth abnormalities have been reported after LSD was injected into rats.[11] However, there are other scientists who hold that there is no conclusive proof of these effects in human beings as yet.

(2) *Marijuana (Cannabis sativa).* Of all the hallucinogens, marijuana is the most abused. Though this drug has been known by man for nearly five thousand years, it is the least understood of them all.[12] Marijuana grows in mild climates throughout the world, especially in Mexico, India, Africa, and the Middle East. It grows in the United States, but its potency is not as great as that grown abroad.

Marijuana, popularly called pot, grass, or joint, consists of the crushed leaves and flowering tops of the female hemp plant. Technically it is known as *Cannabis sativa* (from the Latin *cannabis* for "hemp" and *sativa* meaning "planted" or "sown"). It is a hollow, four-cornered stalk with long narrow leaves and sometimes grows to a height of 20 feet. The resin of this plant contains a group of psychotoxins known as cannabinols, the most potent being tetrahydrocannabinols (THC). Hashish, named after the Persian founder of the Assassins in the eleventh century, consists of the pure resin of the female hemp plant. The active principle of *Cannabis sativa* is concentrated in this brownish-colored substance and is the most potent form of marijuana.

Marijuana is usually rolled into a homemade cigarette and smoked. It quickly enters the bloodstream and acts upon the brain and the nervous system. Its effects are usually felt in about fifteen minutes after ingestion and last from three to six hours. The marijuana high can result in a sense of euphoria or be a "bummer," a bad trip. Ordinarily, it produces a state of intoxication with feelings of extreme well-being, hilarity, confusion, a distortion of time and space, anxiety, fear, and a heightened perception of colors, pictures, and music.

Physiological effects induced by marijuana include dizziness, dryness of mouth and throat, loss of bodily coordination, a craving for sweets, and sometimes nausea. Also, there is an increase in heartbeat, redness of eyes, and a lowering of body temperature. Long-term physical effects are not yet known. Heavy smokers of pot consume from six to twelve reefers, or cigarettes, per day. Fortunately, the marijuana smoker finds that too much intake is unpleasant and therefore regulates his dosage. When he takes large amounts he falls into a deep sleep. Marijuana is not a narcotic and therefore does not cause physical dependence. Hence, there are no withdrawal symptoms. The effects wear off in about twelve hours after intake has been stopped.

What are the dangers of smoking marijuana? It may cause psychological dependence. Some deaths directly related to cannabis have been reported.[13] There is a debate about whether or not the use of pot leads to more dangerous drugs. Studies show that most narcotics users previously used marijuana,[14] but a direct causal relationship has not been proved. Perhaps persons predisposed to abuse one drug may be likely to abuse stronger drugs. The pot user may drop into the drug subculture where he will meet users of hard drugs and be persuaded to experiment with them. Also, here he will meet pushers of a variety of drugs. If pot is not available, he may use the drugs that are for sale. Or he may become dissatisfied with the pleasure derived from cannabis and go on to harder drugs.

(3) *Mescaline.* Mescaline, also called peyote, mescal buttons, or beans, is another hallucinogen. This drug comes from the top of the mescal cactus plant. It contains a white crystalline alkaloid and causes color hallucinations. Hence, it resembles LSD and has a cross-tolerance with this drug. (A person who has developed a tolerance of one will be tolerant of the other.)

When ingested, peyote may cause anxiety, confusion, tremors, euphoria, and depression. It also results in dilated pupils, increased heart rate and blood pressure. The experience is much like that derived from LSD, but it generates less nausea and other side effects.

It is usually ingested in the form of a soluble crystalline powder, which is dissolved or in a capsule. Effects appear within two or three hours and last from four to twelve hours. Some Mexican Indians who descended from the Aztecs still use it in religious worship and for medical purposes.

Peyote or mescaline does not induce physical dependence and therefore no withdrawal symptoms occur upon discontinuance, but psychic dependence may occur.

In the United States, mescaline is authorized for use only for members of the North American Church, which is composed of several thousand Indians who use it as a sacrament in their worship services.[15]

(4) *The Sacred Mushroom (Amanita muscaria)*. The intoxicating properties of certain mushrooms have been known for centuries. The alkaloid, technically called psilocybin, produces a hallucinogenic experience. The most widely used of the mushrooms is the *Psilocybe mexicana*, which grows in marshy pastures. Some Indians use them in their religious worship.

Mescaline, LSD, and psilocybin produce similar experiences. The initial reaction of psilocybin begins within fifteen minutes with mild anxiety which becomes definite in thirty minutes. Perception is altered, vision blurred, and hearing becomes more acute. After an hour, the reaction is definite. There is a sense of euphoria often accompanied by gales of laughter. Then come visions of brilliant colors and shapes which last four or five hours followed by physical and mental depression and a loss of time and space perception.[16]

As for physical changes, psilocybin causes an elevation of body temperature, dilation of the pupils, increased blood pressure and respiratory rate. Although the use of psilocybin does not result in physical dependence, it may cause psychic dependence.

Incidentally, the mushroom that Alice nibbled in Wonderland had hallucinatory properties. After ingesting a bit of it, Alice felt a violent blow underneath her chin. It had fallen down on her foot! She was frightened, felt herself shrinking. Another nibble of the mushroom and she began to grow tall, couldn't find her shoulders, for her neck seemed to rise like a stalk out of a sea of green leaves far below her. She appeared to be a snake.

It is no accident that Lewis Carroll, the author of *Alice in Wonderland,* described Alice on a hallucinogenic trip. He had read about the effects of the *Amanita* mushroom in a review of M. C. Cooke's *British Fungi* from the *Gardener's Chronicle and Agriculture Gazette* of October, 1862.[17]

e. Narcotics   1646751

Generally the term "narcotic" (from the Greek *narkōtikos,* "benumbing") refers to pain-killing drugs of the opium family. These opiates (morphine, codeine, laudanum, narcotine, and others) are derived from opium, the milky substance of the unripe pods of the poppy. This poppy juice is dried to form a brownish gummy material. Opium has been used at least since the days of Homer, who refers to a drug of "sleep and forgetfulness" in *The Odyssey.* As a result of the Opium War (1839–1842), the British forced the Chinese government to legalize opium. Chinese emigrants brought the opium habit with them to the United States and introduced opium smoking. It is sometimes eaten, but mainly smoked in a pipe.

When ingested, opium relieves pain, produces a sense of euphoria, and reduces tension, anxiety, and fear. Its long-term use results in physical dependence.

Morphine (from Morpheus, god of dreams) is derived from opium and is a much abused drug. It consists of 10 percent opium and is a pain-killer. It was discovered in 1803, and during the Civil War many soldiers became addicted to the drug because it was used freely and indiscriminately for pain and surgery. Hence, addiction to morphine became known as the "Soldier's Illness."

Morphine is more addicting than opium. Its physiological results include constriction of the pupils of the eyes, nausea, constipation, itching of the nose and face, flushing of the skin, respiratory depression, sweating, and the lowering of the temperature of the body.

Psychologically, this drug produces drowsiness, mental distortion, weakened sex urge, diminished hunger drive, and mental impairment. Sometimes the drug stimulates apathy and euphoria. Morphine produces physical dependence, and tolerance may develop after three weeks of daily ingestion.

Heroin is another opiate and is derived from morphine. Developed in 1898 by the Bayer Company in Germany, the drug was used to reduce pain and coughing. It is a white, odorless, crystalline powder which dissolves in water. It comes from poppies grown in Turkey, Mexico, and Southeast Asia. Five percent heroin is considered a good quality. Heroin has numerous slang names such as horse, H, smack, junk, hard stuff, joy powder, and scar (from scars or "tracks" as a result of needle injections). Users of heroin are called junkies.

Usually, heroin is injected intravenously with a hypodermic needle (mainlining), though it may be sniffed through the nose (sniffing), or taken by subcutaneous injection (skin popping). In preparation for the dosage, heroin is measured in a teaspoon. Water is added to make the ingredients dissolve quickly. Then it is "cooked" by a cigarette lighter or a candle. When the cooking is done, the liquid is drawn through a ball of cotton, to strain out impurities, into a hypodermic needle, usually an eyedropper with a needle attached. A tourniquet, usually a belt, held by the teeth, is applied to the arm to make the veins more prominent in order to facilitate injection.

Heroin users report that immediately after injection they are "hit" by a warm, glowing sensation centering in the stomach, which spreads all over the body and could be compared only to a sexual orgasm.[18] There is a reduction of tension, anxiety, and fear. The feeling of being high lasts only a short time, followed by depression, nervousness, and a reduction of the sex drive. This state cannot be relieved without another injection of the drug. The heroin addict tends to neglect his health because the drug reduces hunger. Hence, malnutrition is common among addicts. Chronic bronchitis may also occur because heroin deadens the cough reflex. It is estimated that heroin addiction cuts ten to twenty years from the life-span.

Heroin is a dangerous drug. Addiction to this drug is inevitable if one uses it only a few times. The tolerance level is great. To get the same level of high, dosage must be continually increased. An overdose (OD) can result in death. The addict always runs this risk because he does not know what percentage of heroin is in a dose. About eighteen hours after the drug has been discontinued, withdrawal symptoms appear, including shaking, sweating, chills, diarrhea, nausea, abdominal cramps, leg cramps, and mental anguish. The addict must have another shot to relieve his misery.

Heroin addiction is an expensive habit. The cost may run from $35 to $100 per day, depending on the availability of the drug. Feeding this "monkey on the back," or habit, is therefore costly and may lead to a life of chronic crime.

CHAPTER 3

DYNAMICS OF DRUG ABUSE

IN THE STORY of the blind men who encountered an elephant, each tried to deduce its characteristics on the basis of his own "discovery." One of the men fell against the elephant's side and concluded that it was like a wall; another, feeling its tusks, said it was like a spear; the third took hold of the elephant's squirming trunk and declared it to be a snake; the fourth touched its leg and asserted that it was like a tree; the fifth felt its ear and said it was like a fan; the sixth seized its tail and decided it was a rope.

> And so these men of Indostan
> Disputed loud and long,
> Each in his own opinion
> Exceeding stiff and strong,
> Though each was partly in the right,
> And all were in the wrong! [1]

To try to assess the causative factors in drug abuse leaves one in much the same quandary as the blind men. It is never easy to simplify a multidimensional problem. However, in order to delve into specific reasons why the so-called "typical middle-class white young people" use drugs, interviews were conducted with six high school students in Louisville. In response to the direct question, "Why do you use drugs?" the following responses were recorded: "Coping with everyday life is 'yuk,' too much of a hassle." "It puts you in a good place—always makes me happy, enjoy things more. Puts your head in a good place." "Some of my friends told me, you know, and it was really true, said I'd dig it, and I dug it." "Because I didn't like the way things were. I didn't feel I was getting any good out of nothing. Drugs help me a lot." "If you are light, you know, if, like everything is okay, I mean, you know, you are feeling good, you know, you don't have anything to worry about, you don't care what anybody thinks." "I was just lost for things. Looking for something." "Because of my parents." "It just puts your head in a real nice place, where I want to be." "I talked to people and they said it opened them up, so I thought I would try it."

Of the above interviews all except one declared that school pressures were a factor in drug use. Not one of them felt any sense of guilt for taking drugs. None wanted to quit. All indicated that their sources for drugs were both inside and outside the school.

Responses to a questionnaire by 296 high school students from New Albany, Indiana; Louisville, Kentucky; Washington, D.C.; New Orleans, Louisiana; and Pompano, Florida, indicate what these persons think about why students are on drugs. Four percent of the total number interviewed admitted that they were on drugs. Twenty-five percent of the sample indicated the following reasons: "escape from their problems"; "solves problems of loneliness"; "a way out of depression"; "for those

who cannot cope with life"; and "basic insecurities."
Thirteen percent of the sample gave the following reasons: "popularity"; "because we need a group"; "peer
pressure"; "it's the thing to do"; and "to be one of the
crowd."

Eleven percent of the group reported that young
people take drugs because of "curiosity"; "for experimentation"; "just to experience something new."

Fourteen percent of the sample declared: "to turn on";
"for kicks"; "for fun"; "for pleasure"; "makes us feel
happy"; "puts us in a groove "; and "to get a thrill."

All six high school students interviewed and those
surveyed articulate some of the basic reasons why so
many youths are on drugs. (Other interviews and sur-
veys which this writer has supervised through seminary
students report the same reasons.) Some of these psychosocial factors in drug use and abuse are discussed below.

1. Some Purely Personal Factors

Although it is difficult to separate with precision the
personal and social factors of drug abuse, there do appear
to be these two general dimensions of the problem: personal and social. First, here are some of the more personal
factors.

Escapism appears as a contributing element in many
drug abusers. One of the interviewees put it: "Coping
with everyday life is 'yuk,' too much of a hassle." Caught
in the hurricane of social change, youth seek refuge in
the calm eye of the storm. Drug usage for them provides
a passage to shelter from the fierce winds of social reality
and change. Drugs "make the world easier to deal with,"
said one student. Another declared, "Drugs help me a

lot, like you don't have anything to worry about and you don't care what anybody thinks."

Drugs offer these young people a world of less anxiety and fear. They blot out the turmoil of the real world and usher the users into an artificial paradise. So they cop out and retreat behind a chemical curtain. In popular parlance, they "turn on, tune in, and drop out" of the world of reality.

It is interesting to note that some of the students interviewed protested that they did not use drugs to escape from reality. Rather, it was to escape *to* reality. Individuals in a lower economic class tend to use drugs to escape *from* reality (poverty, sordid living conditions, etc.), while those of the upper and middle class do so in order to escape *to* reality (mind expansion, mystical experience, etc.).

Curiosity is another motivation or dynamic for the use of drugs. Our whole educational system is geared to encourage experimentation, to find out things for ourselves. This is true in relation to drugs. As one student put it, "My friends smoked pot and dropped acid and I wanted to try it myself to see what it was like."

Fortunately, the vast majority of those who find out for themselves what drugs are like are experimenters. Out of curiosity they try drugs a few times and then quit. Unfortunately, some young people will, out of curiosity, "try anything once." In the spring of 1969, seven Jefferson County, Kentucky, teen-agers were rushed to hospitals after "flying high" on a tobaccolike drug. Sold in drugstores, the substance usually comes in cigarette form and is smoked for relief by asthmatics and persons with respiratory ailments. These teen-agers had been eating it! One of them had to stay in the hospital ten days and

several others required psychiatric help after being released. The high apparently was caused by the presence
of belladonna, a mild narcotic, and these young people
were probably attracted by a statement on the container
that the drug was 3 percent belladonna. A narcotics
officer reported that the students ate the drug because
"they just try different things and experiment with them
looking for a 'high.' " [2]

A low self-image sometimes leads to drug abuse.
Youths often feel that they are big zeroes when off of
drugs. A sense of inadequacy and inferiority plagues
such persons. For example, a pretty eighteen-year-old
high school dropout, on drugs for three years, explained
why she was a user. She said: "Basically, I was unhappy.
Drugs are a form of escape. I had an inferiority complex
and I just didn't like myself." Being on drugs is "hard to
describe, but it's like you can be anything you want." [3]

Low self-esteem roots in a lack of individual achievement. Dr. David Ausubel thinks that it is caused by the
impairment of motivational maturity as a result of certain childhood experiences. Parents often set goals and
make demands beyond the child's capacity. Drugs provide an escape from this intolerable situation.[4]

Drugs sometimes are used for recreation, and these
recreational users constitute a large portion of the number of users. They feel that being high on drugs, especially marijuana, is appropriate for attendance at con-
certs, movies, and parties because it seems to make these
experiences more enjoyable as their perceptions are
heightened (and distorted). Aesthetic appreciation is
their primary motive for using psychedelics.

James Carey has described the recreational user's style
of life as critical, open-minded, and sensitive. Although

these users are disillusioned with the Establishment, they are not at the point of wanting to "get out." Risks in buying or selling drugs are seldom taken. They recognize the need for law and authority. Politically, they are left of center, nonviolent, and opposed, not to all wars, but to the one in Vietnam.[5] Recreational users are critical of the "straight society" as well as of the hippies whom they consider lazy and unambitious. They agree with other pot smokers that pot should be legalized just as alcohol is, for they substitute marijuana for the martini. The pot party takes the place of the cocktail party.

Many young people are sometimes overwhelmed by a sense of meaninglessness. Life just doesn't make sense for them. In their search for meaning, they turn to drugs. A nineteen-year-old youth got hooked on LSD. Before committing suicide, he dictated his experiences with this chemical into a tape recorder. Among other things, he said:

I have thought it over many times and there really isn't anything to live for. I don't think there is. And I really don't think anyone could convince me that there is . . . not me anyway.[6]

A sense of meaninglessness leads to severe depression. A person may become addicted in an attempt to reduce this state of mind. Depression may be due to anything that threatens personal security—loss of a loved one, finances, job, and reputation. Drugs diminish this sense of loss and help the user to eliminate a depressed feeling. Obviously drugs provide only temporary relief, and once off drugs, the user again becomes depressed.

Man is a creature in a search for meaning. He has a will to meaning, and a sense of meaningfulness is not to be found in mere motion in an affluent culture. As Dr. Sidney Cohen says: "The current problem can be seen as a disease of affluence and non-direction. . . . Freedom from want has produced a vacuum of time which must be filled with meaningful activities, not time-consuming activities." [7]

Hunger for direct emotional and mystical experience propels some to drugs. These experiences are difficult to come by in a rationalistic milieu. The rise of the "death of God" theology, secularized Christianity, impotent and dead institutions, and extreme nationalism tend to rule out both emotional and mystical experiences. Religious and national symbols no longer evoke from many a feeling of elation and pride.

Efforts to revive a feeling for transcendence, faith in terms of liturgical experimentation, modern translations of the Bible, new forms of the church, and religious activism do not meet the needs of those who hunger for individual and religious experience of the kind which young people seek.

The "new morality" is usually the moral stance of the user of drugs. Here he finds some direct experience in terms of freedom in moral decision-making, the inner direction of life, the stress on love (*agapē*), and the rejection of authoritarianism and legalism. Many drug users are actually "post-new morality" in their ethical concern and outlook, for their morality is grounded not only in the agape ethic of Christ, but also in the compassion of Buddha. The Golden Rule of all the great religions has become a central ethical motif in their moral stance.[8]

Rebellion is one of the characteristic traits of many young people today. They are rebelling against family, the middle-class virtues, the military, the educational system, and the Establishment as a whole. Drugs play a crucial role in this rebellion. The use of drugs is an "overrevolt" or an extreme form of rebellion. Psychedelics provide a "pharmacological sacrament" for rebellion, says James R. Allen, "giving it a social ritual, a camaraderie of guiltless law breaking . . . and an effective medication for the relief of feelings of anger, resentment, and aggression." [9]

One of the really basic dynamics of drug abuse is the search for self-identity. Adjustments to reality are sometimes painful for the adolescent. The physical and emotional challenges are too great and some do not make the passage from adolescence to adulthood. Rather, they remain at the motivational level of an adolescent and are unable to compete in an adult world.

Beyond the problems of adolescence, revolutionary changes have created an "identity crisis" for many young people. Confronted with the tragic war, poverty, racism, adult hypocrisy, and a computerized culture, many young people have broken step with the Establishment to pause and query, "Who am I?" and "What am I to do?" Told by parents and the educational system that they live in the greatest democracy on earth "with liberty and justice for all," these youth perceive a credibility gap. They question this legacy and reject the identity that has been handed to them. Feeling that the system cannot be changed to conform to their ideals, some seek to escape through drugs. Failing to discover self-identity in the outer world, they seek it in the inner sanctuary of the self, hoping to find a "cool place" to put their heads.

2. SOCIOLOGICAL FACTORS

Among the sociological forces contributing to the drug epidemic are inadequate family relations, peer-group pressure, mass media, rock music, and an oppressive society.

"Why are you on drugs?" "Because of my parents. They don't understand me and they won't listen," replies the high school youth. Inadequate family relations constitute a major factor in drug abuse. Communication between parent and child is sometimes difficult. Parents deaf-ear the son or daughter and vice versa. Dialogue degenerates into a diatribe with neither parent nor child hearing the other. Parental attention is secured by the children's turning on with drugs. This is a means of punishing the parents and of keeping them "uptight."

Peer-group pressure is one of the most powerful motivational patterns in drug abuse. "My friends turned me on." "I wanted to be accepted in the group." These are familiar statements to every interviewer of youth on drugs. A young person feels a deep need to be included in his peer group. A fourteen-year-old girl declared: "I don't know if I would have been accepted by my friends if I hadn't used drugs. My feelings are that I wouldn't have been. I wanted to be like them." [10]

The use of drugs is the "rite of passage" into the peer group. The youth who will use the most dangerous or exotic drug is seen as the hero, the brave one. Dr. Eugene Schoenfeld, who has treated young addicts in San Francisco, asserts that:

There is a growing use of heroin among young people because young people tend to value the respect of their peers above anything else. Taking the most dangerous drug you can find is a way of gaining that respect.[11]

Peer-group values are powerful and in this social unit traditional moral principles tend to be weakened and ignored. One of the "rites of passage" into the group is the repudiation of middle-class virtues and the values of "square adults." To counter peer-group pressure, Dr. Judianne Densen-Gerber, founder of Odyssey House in Manhattan, New York, suggests: "We've got to have enough children to start a massive healthy adolescent peer-group reaction against drugs." [12]

The mass media have come under attack for not providing a positive approach to the drug problem. Dr. Vincent Lynch, professor of pharmacology at St. John's University, speaking to the Narcotics and Dangerous Drugs Institute in Denver (February, 1970), charged that the mass media have not done their part in alleviating the problem of drugs. Much of the published information, he declared, is not factual and not accurate. At the same institute, Dr. Edward R. Bloomquist, associate clinical professor of surgery at the University of Southern California School of Medicine, provided specific examples of misinformation appearing in the news media about drugs. One example relates to news stories about the experimental drug L-dopa used in the treatment of Parkinson's disease. He noted that although it was played up as an aphrodisiac for older people, the fact that twelve times more patients experienced a psychotic reaction from L-dopa was not reported.[13]

Some feel that certain articles in popular magazines are so presented as to inform the public about drugs but also to encourage their use. Such articles, it is charged, sell not only magazines but also drugs. Manufacturers of illegal drugs and pushers get millions of dollars' worth of free advertising in some of these magazines. Although it may not be the *intent* of these publishers to promote the use of drugs, in actuality, they do.[14]

It is unfair to make the mass media a scapegoat for drug abuse, but it can be charged that reporters do not always present all the facts. There is a tendency on their part and the part of editors to glamorize the exceptional. "Given ten speakers at a symposium," observes Bloomquist, "nine against the use of the drug [marijuana] and one for it, and the headlines will feature the remarks of the pro-cannabis speaker." [15] This gimmick may sell papers, but it does not fully inform the public. Headline writers should be careful not to report happenings involving drugs so as to arouse the curiosity of youth and to encourage them to experiment with drugs. Bloomquist concludes that "where twenty-five years ago the communications media spread horror stories about the danger of cannabis, these same media, and some new ones, now seem to be contributing to its popularity." [16]

The advertisers of drugs are also being criticized, for some people believe that commercials and ads suggest that drugs are the answer to instant relief from pain and a clear route to instant happiness. Utah's Senator Frank Moss, who took the lead in pushing through the Congressional ban on cigarette advertising on radio and television, now is zeroing in on commercials for tranquilizers, stimulants, sedatives, and pain-killers. Moss cites as examples: "For nervous tension, take Compoz" and "Take Sominex tonight—and sle-e-e-ep." Moss, chairman of the Senate's Consumer Subcommittee, has drafted a resolution that would direct the Federal Trade Commission and the National Institute of Mental Health to determine whether such advertising helps promote the "drug culture." [17]

It is alleged that "rock music" promotes the use of drugs. Certainly much of the drug culture language has been popularized by some rock musicians. Band names reflect the language of the drug culture. Among these are The Lovin' Spoonful (reference to the spoon in which heroin is cooked), and The Jefferson Airplane (instrument for holding a marijuana cigarette when it is burned short).

Some rock songs are filled with references to drugs. Take The Beatles' "I Get High with a Little Help from My Friends." "The Crystal Ship," recorded by The Doors (reference to drugs supplied in white crystal such as Methedrine), makes a plea for another kiss, a flashing chance of bliss, before slipping into unconsciousness. "White Rabbit," recorded by The Jefferson Airplane group, describes the effect of the mushroom on Alice in Wonderland, who became tall and small and who chased the White Rabbit. The song ends with "Feed your head, feed your head."

And there is the popular "Psychedelic Shack," recorded by The Temptations, with such phrases as "where it's at," "where you can do your thing." According to the song, the Psychedelic Shack is a place that will "blow your mind."

Whether these and numerous other songs laden with references to drugs encourage or do not encourage their usage is debatable. No thorough research has been done to determine the issue. However, as has been noted, these songs are replete with psychedelic terminology. Young people do tend to take the rock musicians as models of behavior. They also tend to identify with such performers, and the message of the experience of psychoactive drugs comes through loud and clear. The fact that many rock performers have been arrested for possession of drugs makes their style of life a questionable series of models for young people.

There is no doubt in Timothy Leary's mind as to the role of the rock musicians in the drug movement. He says:

The authentic priests, the real prophets of this great movement are the rock-and-roll musicians. Acid-rock is the hymns, odes, chants of the turned-on love genera-tion. For the first time in history, teen-agers (our new advanced mutant species) have written their own songs, beat their own rhythm, created their own religion.

The work of the psychedelic scholar-politicians (described in this history) is over, with love and confidence we turn our work and our planet over to the young and their prophets, the Beatles, the Byrds, the Rolling Stones, Country Joe and the Fish, Charlie Lloyd, the Monkees, the Beach Boys, the Jefferson Airplane, the Mamas and the Papas, the Grateful Dead, Moby Grape, the Daily Flash, the Doors, Donovan, the Association, Buffalo Springfield, the Animals, Big Brother and the Holding Company, and the Quicksilver Messenger Service and many other ecstatic combinations.[18]

Our repressive society tends to promote the use of drugs. Many young people feel that our present culture inhibits their individuality and expression of feelings. By using drugs they seem to overcome their ego inade-quacies, break through the barriers to brotherhood, shatter their defense mechanisms, and reduce their fears of life and death.

In suburbia the white middle class is affluent, and

parents provide their children with the gadgets of affluence. Their offspring do not have to strive for their own support or work for what they get. Hence, they become bored and fed up with the conventional traditions, goals, and virtues of their parents. These young people "split" with the "straight world" in which they have been reared, set up their own culture, and choose their own standards of behavior.

Among the middle class, the rite of passage into adulthood usually involves the kind of behavior that results in good marks in high school, a college diploma, a job, a family, and a house in the best section of town. Then the process starts all over again. Many young people find the pressures in suburbia to conform to a style of life already determined for them intolerable. Hence, they are dropping out of the straight culture because it is a threat to their individuality, the right to make their own decisions, and to express frankly their feelings about life.

All of this points to the fact that our society does not provide the kind of *Sitz im Leben* in which young people feel they can be themselves. As they view it, this is a society void of meaningful goals, challenging causes, and relevant ethical guides. Our goals are related to status and material values. Children are given everything to live *on* but little to live *for*. Causes are related to petty programs to support the *status quo*. There is little challenge to change unjust patterns of social structures, and most action is directed toward keeping things as they are. Morality consists of the middle-class virtues of, by, and for this class. It is an ingroup morality unrelated to the depersonalizing forces felt by other groups in the community.

Our society is producing a segment of sick persons who

seek instant healing by the use of chemicals. Such persons feel that our structures have become too calcified to provide the kind of flexibility that makes for healthy freedom and the achievement of full personhood.

One father of a young drug dependent has summed up what he thinks the contribution of society is to the drug crisis:

We are all suffering in this age, young and old, ghetto and gilded. Nuclear bombs make us expendable, moon rockets render us insignificant, computers know everything about us and care nothing. Extinction threatens us from fouled air, from moral and physical homicide committed by social and political monoliths. It may be that only tough, plasticized emotions survive. It may be that the young flesh and spirit still sensitive have intuitions of cataclysms the way woolly caterpillars in summer, with their fine hair, are said to anticipate the severity of coming winter cold and grow a protective coating.[19]

To escape the threatening society thousands of young people, metaphorically speaking, are spinning a protective chemical cocoon around themselves and looking within the inner self for salvation.

Some of the dynamics or motivations for drug abuse have been examined in this chapter. As in the case of the blind men and the elephant, we may be partly right and partly wrong in our conclusions. Much more research is needed before the psychosocial drug-inducing factors can be understood adequately. Only then can a more constructive strategy be developed to meet the challenge of the drug crisis.

CHAPTER 4

LEGAL CONTROL OF DRUGS

IT IS STARTLING to learn that up until the end of the first decade of this century, narcotics could be purchased in the United States at pharmacies without a prescription. During the eighteenth and nineteenth centuries, generally speaking, opiates were inoffensive to public morals. Opium was used by large numbers of the middle and upper classes in the United States without a knowledge of its dangers. It was classed along with alcohol. Some physicians even thought it was less harmful than alcohol.

By the turn of the twentieth century, because of the spread of drug abuse, the discovery of physicians of the dangers of opium, and press reports, there was a growing public concern about the use of drugs. By 1912 almost every state in the union and numerous cities had enacted laws regulating opiates. Though not rigidly enforced, these laws marked the beginning of the effort to control drugs at the state and local levels.

1. FEDERAL CONTROL OF DRUGS

Growing concern regarding the widespread use of narcotics prompted Congress to pass the Harrison Act of

1914. It required all persons dealing in drugs to register with the Director of Internal Revenue, to pay an occupational tax, and to keep records of narcotics in their possession. It further specified that only "qualified practitioners" (dentists, physicians, veterinarians, surgeons) in pursuit of their professional practice could dispense narcotics, and that druggists could sell them only by written prescription issued by a qualified practitioner.

The Harrison Act has been tested at points by court decisions. A court decision ruled it illegal for a doctor to prescribe narcotics to an addict to relieve withdrawal symptoms, but the Supreme Court modified the decision and implied that the physician should be the judge of what drugs and how many dosages he prescribed for the patient if he did so in good faith. However, a number of doctors trying to walk this fine legal line found themselves arrested for giving drugs to addicts. Some were arrested for overprescribing. Hence, doctors ceased to treat addicted persons.

When the Harrison Act was put into effect, it was assumed that the various states would accept the responsibility for investigating and preventing the local illicit drug traffic by the retail seller and the institutional care of the addict. However, few states initiated any effective plans to enact and to enforce laws against the drug traffic. Hence, in 1932 the Uniform Drug Act was passed. It prohibits any person from manufacturing, possessing, selling, purchasing, prescribing, administering, or giving away any drug except as provided by the act. It further provides for licensing manufacturers and wholesalers of drugs. In short, the act restricts legitimate traffic to qualified manufacturers, wholesalers, drugstores, practitioners, and researchers only.[1]

The Marijuana Tax Act of 1937 placed the same type of controls over marijuana as the Harrison Act did over narcotics. (Marijuana is not a narcotic, but is treated as such under this act.) The act provides that sales of marijuana must involve the payment of a transfer tax of $1 per ounce in legitimate sales and $100 per ounce if sold to illegal purchasers, that is, those who have not registered under the act and paid the special tax. In 1970 this law was imposed upon several young people who came to Newton County, Indiana, to harvest marijuana. The U.S. Internal Revenue Service has been sending tax bills, one as high as $47,800, to youths convicted of possessing the harvested pot.

In 1951, the Boggs Amendment provided mandatory minimum sentences for all narcotic and marijuana offenses: two years for the first offense, five years for the second, and ten years for the third and subsequent offenses. Suspended sentences and probation were prohibited for second offenders. With the passage of the Narcotic Drug Control Act of 1956, the minimum sentences were raised to five years for the first offense and ten years for the second and subsequent offenses for illegal sale or importation, with no possibility of probation or parole. Although the penalties remained the same for unlawful possession, suspension of sentence, probation, and parole were prohibited for all first offenders of unlawful possession.

At the beginning of the 1960's, attitudes began to change toward drug abuse. Increasingly, the drug user was looked upon as a sick person rather than a fiend or vicious criminal. The mass media's somewhat sympathetic attitude toward this view, along with the White House Conference on Narcotics and Drug Abuse in 1962, helped to convey to the public the plight of the addict in terms of a person who needs care and understanding. Even the law enforcers began to see the drug abuser as a victim to be pitied as well as a criminal to be punished.

With the widespread abuse of nonnarcotic drugs (hallucinogens, barbiturates, and amphetamines) in the mid-1960's, Congress passed the Drug Abuse Control Amendments in 1965. They require registration on an annual basis of manufacturers and distributors of these drugs. Physicians prescribing and pharmacists selling must record all prescriptions and sales for three years. Until these laws were passed, drug prescriptions could be refilled without limitation if authorized by a physician. The Drug Abuse Control Amendments state that prescription drugs may not be filled more than five times nor for more than a period of six months without authorization of the doctor, obtained after the fifth refill or subsequent to the expiration of the six months' period. Before this time a doctor could write the letters "p.r.n." on a prescription and it could be refilled whenever the patient so desired.[2]

We find that little research is going on with reference to hallucinogenic drugs. These drugs are not (legally) to be available for student use in university laboratories. Authorized access is available only to a select group of qualified investigators who have the approval of the Food and Drug Administration.

Penalties for violating the law governing nonnarcotic drugs are fairly severe. A first offense is considered a misdemeanor. If the offender is convicted, he is subject to one year in prison or a fine of $1,000, or both. For a second offense, one may be imprisoned up to three years or given a fine up to $10,000. Any person eighteen years or older who sells or gives away these drugs to a person under twenty-one is subject to imprisonment up to two years or a fine up to $5,000, or both. For the second offense or conviction, one may be imprisoned for not more than six years or given a fine of not more than $15,000, or both.

According to the Drug Abuse Control Amendments, no person may possess any depressant or stimulant drugs except for his own personal use or that of a member of his family. If a person is arrested with a hallucinogenic drug in his possession, he is subject to no conviction until it is established that the drug was for sale or to be given to someone else. Although the drug may be confiscated by the legal authorities, the individual cannot be prosecuted for possession.[3]

In 1968 the Dangerous Drug Penalty Amendments were enacted into law. They call for stiffer penalties against illegal manufacture and traffic in hallucinogens, depressant and stimulant drugs, as well as possession of such drugs for sale or disposal to another. This law also makes it a misdemeanor to possess these drugs even for one's own use or other purposes unless prescribed by a licensed practitioner.[4]

At the same time the Dangerous Drug Penalty Amendments were passed in 1968, President Johnson, by executive order, established the Bureau of Narcotics in the Treasury Department with the Bureau of Drug Abuse Control in the Department of Health, Education, and Welfare. This new agency was placed in the Department of Justice and under the Attorney General. Some feel that it was illogical to place the new agency in the Justice Department, concluding that the government's attitude toward drug abuse is punitive rather than preventive.

A tough bill (H.R. 18583) was passed by Congress and signed by the President in 1970. Called the Comprehensive Drug Abuse Prevention and Control Act, this law is designed to produce an intensified federal attack on the illicit use and traffic in drugs. It classifies drugs into five major categories according to their abuse potential. Also, it provides the Attorney General with greater control over the manufacture, distribution, and importation of drugs.

In this new law the penalty structure is revised for drug offenses, eliminating mandatory minimum sentences for all but illegal producers and pushers. Possession of drugs for one's own use, for example, is reduced from a felony to a misdemeanor, with penalties up to one year in prison or a fine of $5,000, or both, for the first offense, with immediate probation possible. A second offense is judged to be a felony. Penalties for professional pushers are set at up to twenty-five years in prison and fines up to $200,000.

The law also contains a "no knock" provision (Sec. 509 (b)). It provides that agents can go before a magistrate and get a warrant if they can demonstrate to the magistrate that the evidence will be destroyed or the officer's life will be put in danger if he has to announce his entry. This authority is restricted to special agents of the Bureau of Narcotics and Dangerous Drugs. A main argument for the "no knock" law is the claim that peddlers in drugs flush them down toilets before the knock of an agent is answered.

Some fear that this law will undermine the Constitution and the principles upon which the great calling of the law rests. When the bill was being debated in Congress, Senator Sam Ervin declared that both Democrats and Republicans tried to be "so zealous in their efforts to enforce the law that they would emulate the example set by Samson in his blindness and destroy the pillars upon which the temple of justice itself rests." [5]

2. STATE LAWS AND DRUGS

State laws are so varied and numerous that it is impossible even to list them in this study. However, there is a trend in the states toward a more lenient attitude toward the drug abuser and heavier punishment for the pusher. In the last three or four years, more than twenty-five states have revised their laws to soften the harsh penalties for marijuana possession and usage. Generally the changes reduce the penalty for first convictions for the possession of pot. Too, these laws provide the judges with greater flexibility and latitude in dealing with first offenders. However, second offenders and pushers continue to face stiff penalties.

Kentucky is an example of how public opinion can modify laws against marijuana. The new law of 1970 removed marijuana from being classified as a narcotic to the category of dangerous drugs. Under the old law, conviction for selling or disposing of a dangerous drug called for a prison sentence of two to five years, or a fine of $1,000 to $5,000, or both. The new law removes the minimum fine and sentence, but provides for a sentence of up to ten years, or $10,000, or both, for subsequent convictions. Conviction for possession of marijuana for personal use is classified as a misdemeanor rather than a felony. Second and subsequent convictions are classified as felonies. Treatment and rehabilitation at a mental health facility designated by the Department of Mental

Health is mandatory for each first offense. If the offender is unwilling to participate in the treatment, he goes back to the court, and a fine up to $600 and/or imprisonment in the county jail for up to six months may be imposed. A second offense could bring a one-year jail sentence and a fine of $1,000. Third and subsequent offenders could get up to five years in prison and a fine of $5,000. However, the law does not take away any authority of the judge to probate offenders.

Under the new Kentucky law, conviction for selling dangerous drugs to a minor brings a heavy penalty. This act is classified as a felony, and a fine up to $20,000 and/or imprisonment up to ten years may be imposed.

3. INTERNATIONAL DRUG CONTROL

At the international level, most governments are getting tougher rather than more lenient about the use and sale of marijuana. The Single Conventions Treaty of 1961 requires that the United States, along with seventy-three nations of the World Health Organization, seek to curb the traffic in dangerous drugs, including marijuana. The treaty's goal is to eliminate the use of cannabis in member countries in the next twenty-five years. Both legal and educational methods are to be used in this program.[6]

The United States is stepping up its efforts to stem the tide of dangerous drugs flowing into this country from Turkey, Mexico, and Southeast Asia. Heavy pressure is being put on Turkey to end the legal poppy crop, but with small success. The Bureau of Narcotics and Dangerous Drugs now has 850 agents, but this number is sadly inadequate. In New York, where the inflow of heroin is the greatest, the government has only fifteen customs officials at the airports and the waterfront.[7]

Open season has been declared in Turkey, Lebanon, Morocco, Spain, France, and other countries on American amateur smugglers of drugs. Some 550 American youths are awaiting trial or serving up to eight years in prison in thirty-seven foreign countries on drug charges. Most of these young people are arrested when they attempt to cross borders with drugs.

Fair warning has been issued to Americans abroad about the danger of being caught with drugs. The hippie type is a prime target for a thorough search by the police in foreign countries. A reporter who toured the hashish trail abroad has some good advice for amateur smugglers:

If you buy drugs, be prepared for the man who sells them to you to be a police informer or even a cop.
Don't sell any drugs.
Don't give them away, either—that's distribution or trafficking.
Don't cross frontiers with drugs.
Foreign jails are especially unpleasant.[8]

It should be added also that American Consulate Generals in these countries can provide no help for the drug offender.

4. MARIJUANA: SHOULD IT BE LEGALIZED?

A heated debate is now in process as to whether or not marijuana should be legalized. Politicians and professors, specialists and laymen, are arguing the pros and cons of legalization. As we have seen, there is a trend at

both federal and state levels to modify cannabis laws
with emphasis on softening the penalties for possession
of the drug and increasing them in regard to the pusher
and the illicit producer. Public opinion in general appears to favor this trend. But there are those pro-cannabis proponents who insist that all laws against pot
should be eliminated.

Proponents who advocate making marijuana legal
point out that a large number of Americans are using
the drug, that it has become a new social practice among
the middle class, and that its use is becoming more widespread in spite of laws against it. A comparison of the
present situation and the Prohibition era is made. Prohibition, they observe, did not work with reference to
alcohol, and laws against pot will not be effective, either.
It is argued that laws which do not have the support
of the people will not be obeyed and attempts to enforce
such laws only encourage violation and contempt for
them.

Anti-cannabis legalization exponents note that actually only a few people use marijuana. While twenty
million may have tried the drug, only about 3 to 5 percent use it with any regularity.

This brings up another argument for legalizing pot.
Some argue that alcohol is a greater health hazard than
marijuana. Six million people are hopelessly hooked on
alcohol. One half of the deaths caused by auto accidents
are related to drinking drivers. The pro-cannabis people
point out that marijuana has none of these disastrous
results. Hence, there is a double standard by which alcohol is defended and marijuana is attacked. Adults appear to be hypocritical or inconsistent in condemning
one form of drug while indulging in another that is

thought to be more harmful. It is argued that marijuana violations should be treated in the same way as alcohol violations.

On the con side of the debate, there are those who note that alcohol does have some medical value apart from intoxication. Marijuana, so far as is known, has no medicinal use. Moreover, marijuana, like alcohol, distorts one's vision and coordination and may lead to accidents. Alfred R. Lindesmith, who is pro-cannabis in the cannabis-alcohol debate, admits that it is "undeniable that marijuana intoxication may sometimes lead to automobile accidents and to irresponsible criminal acts." [9] Thus, it is pointed out, we cannot afford to put pot in the same category with alcohol to become another destructive burden upon our society. Although the charge of inconsistency in the laws against marijuana and alcohol is true, this does not justify the adoption of a new vice by trying to show that it is no worse than another one. Former director of the U.S. Food and Drug Administration, Dr. James L. Goddard says:

If the *known* harmful effects of alcohol and tobacco are greater than those of marijuana, and those substances are legal, why do I not advocate legalizing marijuana? I believe that if alcohol and tobacco were not already legal, we might very well decide *not* to legalize them—knowing what we now know. In the case of marijuana, we will know in a very few years how harmful it is or is not. If it turns out to be relatively harmless, we will be embarrassed by harsh laws that made innocent people suffer. If it turns out to be quite harmful—a distinct possibility —we will have introduced yet another public health hazard that for social and economic reasons might become impossible to dislodge.[10]

And as Dr. Donald B. Louria notes, "Our society has opted for enough escape mechanisms already—liquor, caffeine, cigarettes." [11] What is needed is a consistent effort to control alcohol and to eliminate the evils associated with it.

There is the disputation about whether the use of marijuana leads to harder drugs. On the pro-pot side it is held that there is no causal relationship between the use of marijuana and other more potent drugs. Dr. John E. Ingersoll, director of the Federal Bureau of Narcotics, admits that the "overwhelming majority" of the chronic users of marijuana do not go on to other drugs. However, he quickly notes that the overwhelming majority of those who use heroin or LSD in the United States and England had previous experience with marijuana or hashish.[12] The Bureau of Narcotics claims that 75 to 80 percent of the heroin addicts in this country began their drug use with marijuana.

Although there may be no actual causal factor between the use of marijuana and harder drugs, there are circumstances which may lead in this direction. Due to the fact that marijuana is outlawed, the user is sometimes thrown into the drug subculture where he meets pushers of all kinds of drugs. If pot is not available, the pusher may urge the user to try something else such as speed (amphetamines) or even heroin. It is the conviction of Amitai Etzioni, professor of sociology at Columbia University, that "to the degree heroin rides piggy-back on marijuana, it seems more due to the law than to the pushers; by making both illegal, the law pushes the users of marijuana (at least the distributors) into contact with criminal elements, who control both." [13]

Here Etzioni is hinting at the criminogenic nature of

the law against the use of marijuana. More will be said about this later. The most that can be said at this stage of research is that there is some truth to the charge that marijuana use leads to the use of harder drugs. When the supply runs short, the users of pot are often introduced to the harder drugs and some leave the "kid stuff" and graduate to heroin. Or they may become dissatisfied and/or bored with marijuana and move on to harder drugs. Although only a small percentage do go on to heroin, numerous studies show that from 75 to 90 percent of the heroin users were prior users of the less potent marijuana. As Bloomquist notes:

Nine out of ten heroin users—sometimes more, depending on the study quoted, but never less—used cannabis first. They found it was not sufficient to solve their ego-inadequacies and stepped up to something more suited to their emotional needs.[14]

One of the most popular arguments for the use of marijuana is that it enhances creativity. It is alleged that by the use of this drug one can reach high peaks of creativity in music, art, and literature. This is true, it is argued, because marijuana sharpens one's perception, aiding one in an artistic or literary endeavor. The use of pot frees a person from his hang-ups and inhibitions, enabling him to be more open to reality and to focus upon the present moment. Thus he can perform with greater creativity. Such are some of the rationales for using pot to enhance artistic and intellectual performance. How valid are these claims?

Studies show that instead of increased creativity, marijuana simply removes inhibitions and the "artist" *feels* that he is being more creative. There is no evidence that his performance is improved to any noticeable degree.[15] As for the claim that cannabis enhances one's ability to think more clearly and make top grades, this is a myth. Students who use pot and make high marks are not dependent users. They are what Bloomquist calls the "chippers" and have no compulsive need to relieve tensions. "Unlike the true addict," he says, "they remain in the mainstream of life despite, not because of, their use of the drug" and "continue to be achievement-oriented and competitive."[16]

Indeed, one of the characteristics of the regular user of marijuana is a loss of motivation. The amotivational syndrome includes general apathy, a lack of interest and ambition, and a tendency to become a social cop-out. Richard Lingeman notes that the general prognosis of the heavy marijuana user is that after about twelve years on marijuana he may "mature out" of his habit, but "the slacking of motivation attendant to regular use will cause a loss of twelve years out of his life—enough to blight his entire career."[17] Legalization of pot could produce a nation of unmotivated and unambitious persons. There would be only a limited future for a nation filled with a purposeless people submerged in a drug culture.

Pro-marijuana people do not believe that the use of this drug causes physical or psychological damage.[18] The LaGuardia Report of 1944 is used to sanction this claim. This study was made by the New York Academy of Medicine and reports that marijuana does not alter the basic personality or do any physical damage.[19] It is true that up to now no serious damage to the physical body has been determined by scientists who have studied the effects of marijuana. They have detected an increase of heartbeat and of blood sugar, and basal metabolic elevation in the user. Pupil dilation and redness of the eyes occur, and the skin becomes very sensitive to touch. But no one knows what the long-term effects will be. In India, where cannabis has been used for centuries, Dr. David P. Ausubel reports that 42 percent of chronic users have damaged health in terms of congestion of the eyes, pharyngitis, laryngitis, chronic bronchitis, loss of weight, diarrhea, and depression of sexual activity.[20]

There is no question as to the debilitating psychological effects of marijuana on some users. Bloomquist sums them up:

> But we do know: cannabis may confuse the mind, impair judgment, distort perception, increase suggestibility, weaken will power, and diminish the faculty of self-criticism to the extent that many times the user may arrive at the inaccurate conclusion that he belongs to a superior order of beings. . . . Cannabis can erode ambition, . . . encourage irresponsibility, and remove the individual from the mainstream of life by diminishing or diverting into negative channels creativity which could benefit all society; this is wasted because the user is too busy turning on and ultimately dropping out.[21]

Although this list of effects applies to only a minority group in America, it is sufficient to cause serious concern about the spreading use of marijuana. The long-term effects are not yet known and may prove to be disastrous to a large segment of our society. The risk of marijuana for the individual and society is too great, for it is "a kind of chemical Russian roulette." [22]

Some argue that marijuana laws are too harsh. Others would make the existing penalties heavier. Still others hold that pot should be legalized. The present laws, they contend, are by nature criminogenic, that is, they make criminals and lawbreakers. Moreover, these laws provide harsh criminal penalties for a minor offense. There is, of course, some truth in this, and some states are moving toward more lenient penalties for first offenders, but not for the pusher. President Nixon himself has said: "When you are talking about thirteen-year-olds and fourteen-year-olds and fifteen-year-olds, the answer is not more penalties. The answer is information. The answer is understanding." [23]

There is no doubt that marijuana laws applied to young first offenders are harsh and sometimes cruel. They're often given unrealistic and excessive penalties. For example, Frank LaVarre was arrested for possession of marijuana in Danville, Virginia. He was sentenced to twenty-five years in prison, with five years off for good behavior. Until three weeks before his arrest, he had never tried marijuana. (In Virginia the minimum penalty for possessing more than 25 grains, about half a teaspoonful of marijuana, is twenty years in prison, the same as the minimum penalty for first-degree murder.) [24] In some states, Georgia, for example, the sale of marijuana to a minor can bring the death penalty.[25]

Co-indictment in marijuana arrests is also an unreasonable and harsh law. If marijuana is found on one person or in an automobile in which two or more are riding, all are co-indicted—this in spite of the fact that only one of the group possessed the drug and none were smoking it. The reason for this is that the "clean" individuals will be charged with being aware that one person in the group possessed the marijuana.[26]

Dr. James L. Goddard has summed up our antiquated legal system with reference to marijuana:

Our laws governing marijuana are a mixture of bad science and poor understanding of the role of law as a deterrent force. They are unenforceable, excessively severe, scientifically incorrect, and revealing of our ignorance of human behavior. The Federal and State laws should be revised to reflect the fact that marijuana is a hallucinogen and should be classified as such. The Federal statutes should be repealed, and the Food, Drug, and Cosmetic Act should be amended to bring marijuana under the jurisdiction of that act, thereby automatically de-escalating the penalties for simple possession to a more reasonable level (a misdemeanor, with the judge being given considerable authority to adjust the penalty to more nearly fit the circumstances). At the same time sufficiently serious penalties should be provided to handle the major traffickers in the drug. State laws should then be revised in conformance with a model law containing similar provisions.[27]

Our laws on marijuana must be updated, humanized, and more adequately enforced. To legalize marijuana may open the door to types of drugs more potent than American-grown pot, such as *mexicanna* and *indica,* and create a large group of drug dependents.[28] To legalize marijuana would also mean an increased number of users. Ferdinand Mount, in reply to a full-page ad in *The London Times* calling for complete repeal of all laws against marijuana, declared:

It is obvious that if marijuana were legal more people would smoke it. More people would therefore be aware of the delight of taking leave of their senses. Anybody who claims that there would be *fewer* people ready to go on to experiment with heroin is operating with an exiguous knowledge of human nature. Did the end of Prohibition bring a significant or lasting reduction of alcoholism? [29]

It is the conclusion of this writer that marijuana should not be legalized. The result would be a pot culture superimposed upon an alcohol culture when we are not even coping adequately with the latter. At the same time, laws should be made more lenient for the first offender and the heavy penalties retained for the pusher. Instead of expending so much time and effort to apprehend the experimenter and casual user, an all-out continuous crusade should be made to eliminate the pusher, the illegal wholesaler, and criminal syndicates which are the major sources of dangerous drugs.

CHAPTER 5

PARENTS AND THE DRUG PROBLEM

Two weeks ago, my beautiful twenty-year-old daughter leaped to her death from her apartment while she was in a depressed suicidal frame of mind, believing in panic that she was losing her mind from recurring bad trips from an LSD experiment some six months before.

That her death was a shock to the family and to the nation goes without saying. I made the decision that her tragic death would not be hushed up, it would not be covered over as is the case with so many prominent children and people; but that I would seek to shock the nation into the realization that this is not happening to other people's children in some poor part of the town. It can happen to a well-educated, intelligent girl from a family that has traditionally been a Christian family and has been straight.[1]

The shock of tragedies similar to that of the Art Linkletter family is being felt in thousands of homes of our society. In the midst of their anguish, grief-stricken parents and relatives are asking plaintively: "What did we do wrong? Where did we fail? What can we do *now*?"

1. WHAT IS A PARENT TO DO?

Individual reactions vary when parents discover the chilling fact that one or more of their children are dealing in some way with drugs. At first, the usual parental reaction is incredulity. "How could this happen to *us?* What can we do?" The whole problem of drug abuse is so new that few know what positive steps can and should be taken. Admittedly there are no neat formulas to follow. However, there are some guidelines.

For one thing, keep your cool and don't panic. It is difficult to think clearly and make sound decisions when frightened. In this state of mind one may act in such a manner as to worsen the situation. Remember that one of the reasons the youth is on drugs may be to get his parents uptight.

Don't go into a blind rage and beat the offspring or order him out of the house. Such overreaction may impair the family relationship and probably encourage the son or daughter to continue drug use rather than to end it. Punitive attitudes and actions will drive some youth to become more involved in drugs as an act of defiance. At this crucial time the youth needs acceptance, not brutal rejection. To force him out of the house is to push him right into the drug culture and probably into the courts and prison.

Don't turn a youngster on drugs over to the police. This could be one of the most damaging things a parent could do. It may turn the youth permanently against his parents. Among other things, it could mean expulsion from school or even imprisonment where he would get a postgraduate course in real crime. As a youth, he may be the object of abuse by hardened criminals and homosexuals. To be convicted on a drug charge is a felony, and this would mean the loss of basic rights as a citizen. Such a person is stripped of his right to vote, to serve in the military, to hold a government post, and to work in numerous jobs. For example, a licensed barber convicted of a drug violation cannot follow his vocation again.

Instead of calling the police, call a physician and seek his advice and help. Usually he will be sympathetic and know what further step to take. He is familiar with all the resources for treatment and rehabilitation.

The parent is faced with a difficult problem if the youngster is a pusher and will not voluntarily seek help. In this case, the authorities may have to be notified. If he is a junkie and will not seek help, about the only thing parents can do is to kick him out. Otherwise, they will support him and feed his habit, which will get bigger. To continue to support him and coddle him will keep him an infant, a baby, and this is what he wants. He must give up drugs or leave home. But before such a course of action is taken every effort should be made to get the drug abuser and pusher into a hospital or rehabilitation program.

Do not ignore the fact that a child is using drugs. Some parents will simply not face the issue and cannot believe that their children would do such a terrible thing. Ignoring the problem will not make it go away. It cannot be wished away. The sooner the problem is confronted the better. To neglect it may result in the youth's becoming hooked on a drug to the point where little help can be given to get him off it.

Don't try purposefully to frighten children off drugs. They will deaf-ear parents or anyone else who tries this approach. Scare tactics will not work because those on drugs usually know more about their nature and effects than parents do. They know the drug jargon and can outargue their parents. The result will be further alienation.

What has been suggested so far has been in terms of negatives, what not to do. Some positive suggestions are in order as preventive measures.

Parents should become informed about drugs. This means that they will become aware of the nature of drugs, the etiology of drug abuse, and therapeutic measures available for the addicted. This will make it possible for parents to attack the drug problem with facts and to act in the most intelligent manner in dealing with drug abuse.

Communication is essential in coping with the young drug abuser. One of the first things parents should do is to talk openly with their son or daughter. It is a time when parents must demonstrate the fine art of listening as well as giving advice. So listen and don't lecture. The victim of drugs needs to be heard rather than harangued and harassed.

The family relationship should be so structured as to make it possible for children to feel that they will be heard, that parents will hear them out, in the spirit of understanding. This will require an openness of parents and a willingness to reason together. This is the sort of line of communication which should be open at all times between parent and child.

Counseling services are available in most communities. It may be necessary to seek such outside counseling if a drug abuser does not communicate well with his parents. Perhaps the school counselor can provide some assistance. The family physician can give counsel or refer to some competent person who can. A trusted and mature friend (businessman, lawyer, or minister) may be as helpful as some professionals in getting the drug abuser to kick his habit.

Every child needs good parental examples to identify with. This generation of children has been born and reared in a society of drug-oriented parents and households. It is most difficult to persuade children not to use marijuana when they see their parents using alcohol, a drug that has destructive effects on the body and may cause both psychological and physical dependence. It is estimated that eighty million Americans use alcohol and that six million are alcoholics. If alcohol had not been known before our day and were introduced today, it would probably be declared illegal along with other drugs.

Young people are quick to detect a credibility gap between the preachments of parents about drugs and their daily consumption of alcohol. Drinking and tranquilizing middle-class parents are being hypocritical when they berate their offspring for using another drug which may not be as harmful. A child needs models to follow and drug abusers generally have unhealthy ones. In his studies of addicts, Isidore Chein and his co-workers discovered that four out of five addicts had a weak relationship with a father figure. In most cases the mother figure was dominant in the daily life of the child.[2] Studies by P. Zimmering and others come to the same conclusions.[3]

Of course, a child does not necessarily turn to drugs because of poor models or the failure of parents who express either too little or too much love. Some children are able to overcome these early experiences, but the odds are against them. It must be remembered that children "well brought up" can be turned to drugs by their peer group.

Even in families where there is peace, harmony, and love a child may become a drug abuser. As Ira Mothner says, "What you are getting into is a tug of war, parents versus kids, you against the child's buddies, and a good clutch of the nation's psychiatrists are betting on the buddies." [4] But if parents set good examples, their children will have a better chance of resisting the drugs. They will have a moral reserve and the image of personal integrity which they can never completely forget.

2. DETECTING THE DRUG ABUSER

It is most important to detect the child on drugs in the early stage. Chances for saving him from becoming a chemical cop-out will be much greater. Certain signals or tip-offs of drug use are evident in every person.

A child who has done well in school and loses interest in his studies, becomes irregular in attendance, and makes lower marks may be telling us that he has become involved with drugs. Of course, this is not always the case. Nevertheless, parents should check with the school counselor and teachers to find out the basic cause of the child's change of attitude and action. Another sign to take seriously is when a child changes his set of friends. If he suddenly adopts new friends and drops out of the circle of old ones, this should be a matter of genuine concern for parents. Check out these new comrades. Chances are that they will be youths of questionable behavior and involved in the drug culture.

Money becomes a problem for the drug abuser. Drugs cost money and it must come from somewhere. In order to support the habit, allowances will be exceeded. Both money and household items may begin to disappear. When this supply runs out, the youngster may turn to crime, such as shoplifting and petty thievery.

In the area of morality, the drug abuser finds it easier to compromise on ethical issues because drugs decrease one's inhibitions. Drugs increase suggestibility, so that moral problems are more easily solved. Moral principles are shunted aside or compromised in order to feed the monkey on the abuser's back. This comes first in his life, and his attention is focused solely on getting the drug regardless of the moral cost.

Parents should be concerned when a child comes and goes at odd hours of the day and night. This may mean that he is smoking pot with friends in some crashpad, park, or vacant house. Sleeping late during the morning hours may or may not mean that the youngster is using drugs. At any rate, such behavior should be looked into to find out why the child doesn't want to get up in the mornings.

Drugs affect the spirituality of the user. Religious experience may become disoriented. An intense interest in Eastern religions, especially Zen Buddhism, may indicate the use of drugs. The person on drugs tends to give expression to his religious feelings in Eastern religious categories because they are mystical in nature. If the child has one or more statues of Buddha, is reading literature in Eastern religions, and burning incense in his room, it may just be that pot is being used to promote a mystical experience. At the college level, the student on drugs may postpone his choice of a vocation or career. His subjects of interest are usually the humanities, especially philosophy. Such courses as physics, chemistry, medicine, and engineering are shunned. If these druggies make it through the undergraduate school, they opt for graduate study rather than a job and the responsibility of making a living.

The occasional user of drugs is difficult to detect. He may ingest pot or LSD on weekends or two or three times a month. Casual use, as in the case of alcohol, will not necessarily result in psychotic or mental derangement if the user is not psychologically disposed to it.

Physical signs are not very prominent in the occasional user of chemicals. Psychotropics and amphetamines do dilate the pupils of the eyes and may cause a loss of weight. Also, erratic and panicky behavior may be detected in the users of these drugs. Pot causes redness of the eyes, but this can be concealed by dark glasses or reduced by the use of eye drops. Pot has a sweet odor, but incense is burned to banish it. On an LSD trip the individual's face becomes flushed or red and he may betray paranoid tendencies, feeling that he is being persecuted.

The chronic user of drugs, especially heroin, can easily be detected. Persons strung out on heroin will have an emaciated appearance. Look for "tracks" or hypodermic needle scars along the course of the veins in his arms. He will probably wear long sleeves to conceal such marks. Those who "pop," or inject, drugs on the arms, legs, thighs, and abdomen may have scars and abcesses due to infection where a dirty needle has been used to penetrate the skin. The user's eyes will be dilated. Licking of lips, drowsiness, poor coordination, and intoxication are also signs of heroin use. The heroin user may suddenly fall asleep wherever he may be. If he is addicted to the drug and cannot get a "fix" (another dose), he will experience withdrawal symptoms characterized by a running nose, sniffing, sweating, stomach pains, muscle cramps, and perhaps periods of unconsciousness.

Parents must constantly be on the alert for drug abuse among their children. The old idea that "it can't happen here," in our home, is a false one. It happens in the "best" of families. Early detection is essential, and we hope the suggestions in this chapter will be helpful to parents whose homes drug abuse can invade.

CHAPTER 6

RESOURCES FOR REHABILITATION

ONE OF THE TRAGIC ASPECTS of the drug crisis is that there are so few resources available for the rehabilitation of the drug abuser. In most small communities in the United States there are no facilities available at all. Many large cities have few agencies to which those in drug trouble can appeal. The shortage of facilities is understandable because the drug problem has become acute only in the last few years. This chapter will be concerned with some of the redemptive agencies and institutions for drug rehabilitation in the nation.

1. HOSPITALS

The Federal Government operates two large hospitals for addicts. One is at Fort Worth, Texas, and the other at Lexington, Kentucky. Since this writer is more familiar with the hospital in Lexington, the focus of our concern here will be upon this institution. The first patients were admitted in 1935 when it was called the First Federal Narcotics Farm. It was essentially a prison with the patients under guard at all times and with almost no freedom. Windows in the hospital were barred, and patients were not allowed to leave the hospital or to go into the courtyard. At times there were over a thousand beds in use, but there was no therapy program and no program for thorough research on drugs.

In January of 1967, the National Institute of Mental Health took over the Lexington Hospital and it was renamed Clinical Research Center to stress its new role as a model treatment, training, and research facility for problems of drug dependence and abuse. Radical changes were made in its treatment program, basic philosophy, and methods of operation. Bars were removed and the prison atmosphere eliminated. Persons in the hospital are no longer called "patients" but "residents." The Center stopped admissions of voluntary or prisoner patients.

In accordance with the Narcotic Addiction Rehabilitation Act of 1966, a new policy of admittance was adopted. This law provides for the civil commitment of narcotic addicts, including those charged with or convicted of violating federal criminal laws. Hospitalization is provided for a period of six months and for professionally supervised aftercare services in the community for thirty-six months following discharge. Entrance to the Clinical Research Center program is made through the office of the local United States Attorney. Residents now occupy the Center, and they live in small therapeutic communities called "alleys." These are autonomous, separate living areas to facilitate closer resident-staff relationships and to encourage each unit to sponsor its own project. Self-disciplinary meetings, marathon group sessions, and "encounter" sessions are held when one of the community violates the self-composed constitution. Residents select their own community leaders and elect members of the community representative council and the council on resident ethics which act as central representative bodies for both men and women.

Each resident has his own private room and is allowed to decorate it as he wishes. Residents freely share everything that they have, and there is feeling of a real community setting. At certain hours both men and women residents are permitted to gather in the large courtyard for informal fellowship. At the present, there are approximately five hundred residents in this institution. A typical day begins at 6:30 in the morning when all residents are awakened for breakfast, which is served at 7:00 A.M. At 8:00 the residents meet with doctors, psychiatrists, and staff members to talk about problems. At 9:00 the resident assumes his job assignment in vocational therapy: library training, needleshop and sewing center, printshop, kitchen techniques, woodshop, dentist office, data processing, and secretarial.

Lunchtime is at 12:00 noon. At 1:00 P.M. free time begins with recreational therapy: gymnasium, bowling alley, group therapy sessions on grounds, Ping-Pong, picnics, field trips. The evening meal is at 6:00 P.M. followed by encounter meetings at 7:00 P.M., with the attendance of all residents required. At 9:00 P.M. all residents return to the alleys and lights are out at 11:00 P.M.

The Lexington Hospital accepts men residents from states east of the Mississippi River and female patients from all over the United States. The federal hospital in Fort Worth accepts male addicts west of the Mississippi. The majority of the residents are in these institutions because of their abuse of morphine, heroin, meperidine, paregoric, and numorphan. There are a few residents who have been on LSD, marijuana, and glue.

As a part of the new rehabilitation program all residents are individually evaluated several times during their stay. Privileges and rewards are withheld from residents who refuse to work. To maintain a drug-free atmosphere, random urine samples are tested every morning. To motivate residents, incentives and rewards are granted to those who show progress in therapeutic and rehabilitative activities. These include more freedom, special social recreational functions, choice of rooms, and improved vocational opportunities.

Research and treatment are coordinated so that the one will encourage and reinforce the other. The addiction research center continues its investigation and studies of opium abstinence and its treatment, and the relationship of the chemical structure of drugs to addictiveness.

Studies have shown that under the old system 90 percent of the released patients became readdicted, many of them within six months after release from the hospital.[1] It is too early to judge the results of the new program, but both the patients and social workers are optimistic about the program's efficiency.

One of the distinctive features of the new program is that of aftercare. After six months of treatment at the Center the resident enters the aftercare program. This program gives the patient support and supervised care in his home community. It is a flexible program and lasts for approximately thirty-six months. Almost any type of agency can serve as an aftercare center, with counselors from employment bureaus, child-care centers, mental health centers, etc. Each counselor is allowed twenty patients and each patient sees a counselor about once a week. Tests are given periodically to determine whether the patient has returned to the use of drugs.

One of the services provided to the public is that of the guided tour of the Lexington Hospital. Church, school, and civic groups come to learn about the program. After an orientation lecture, visitors are taken on a tour of the hospital and have the opportunity to share dialogue with the residents. A small, but excellent, library is open every day except Sunday for those who wish to do reading and research in the area of drug abuse.

2. SPECIAL CLINICAL TREATMENT CENTERS

Some hospitals around the country have methadone programs. For example, Dr. Gerald Starkey heads up the Hold and Treat Ward in Denver General Hospital, which has a methadone program. This drug is used as a substitute for heroin, opium, and other hard drugs. It costs about two dollars to satisfy the addict's habit each day. Methadone, which was developed in 1962, is substituted for another drug. It has the effect of blocking the craving and the withdrawal syndrome of addictive drugs.

There are arguments pro and con for the use of methadone. It is cheap and takes the drug addict off the streets to the clinic. It eliminates the necessity of stealing to support the habit. It permits the user to go to work and to school and to pursue most other normal activities without the chronic, nagging, common hunger for drugs. The mental processes are virtually unimpaired while under the influence of the drug. Some argue that this drug simply substitutes one form of addiction for another and that its long-term effects are unknown. There is also a danger of overdosage if methadone is not used under strict supervision.

3. REHABILITATION CENTERS

Among the growing number of private and semi-private rehabilitation centers are Logos House, Renaissance House, Synanon, Narcotics Anonymous, Odyssey House, Samaritan Center, Daytop Village, and others. In this section only a few of these can be described.

Narcotics Anonymous was organized in 1948 and is structured along the lines of Alcoholics Anonymous. It follows essentially the same program. However, it has not been too successful for several reasons: discussing drugs in a group may move participants to go out and get "fixed"; pushers may sometimes attend meetings; narcotics squad members infiltrate the group; and addicts are often so dependent that they are unable to provide the strength to maintain the group. Nevertheless, it has had a measure of success with some of the members of the group. Also, there is a companion organization called Nar-Anon for wives and children. In this organization the family learns to understand the drug abuser and how to help him and to live with him.

Some communities now have drug information and education centers. Louisville, Kentucky, has established the Drug Abuse Information and Education Center, Inc., which serves as a coordinating agency for the guidance and rehabilitation programs, as well as for information and educational services for the general public. The office establishes and maintains the necessary contacts with medical, educational, managerial personnel and facilities. Its staff consists of a coordinator, secretary, and several former drug users who serve as volunteers in conducting group sessions with present drug users. It provides twenty-four-hour phone service ("hot line") and a drop-in center to accommodate the experimenter and user. The Center provides a place for young people to go for help without getting "busted" by the police. Arrangements for those needing emergency admittance to the General Hospital's seventy-two-hour program can be handled through this Center. The Center also acts as a contact-information point, where one can make new drug-free friends, and as a facility for runaways until a contact is reestablished with parents and family. Volunteers, including ex-drug users, medical students, and doctors staff the Center twenty-four hours a day. The first floor is used for the Center's current information and educational services. The upper two floors are used for counseling.

A number of centers called halfway houses are being organized across the country to care for drug abusers. Three of these are briefly described.

Synanon was founded by Charles Dederich in 1958 in Santa Monica, California. There are now three hundred addicts living in centers in Santa Monica, San Diego, New Haven, and Nevada State Prison. Synanon's purpose is to achieve "moral regeneration through the process of education." Its program is similar to that of AA. All applicants are screened by older members who are ex-addicts. If accepted, the addicts are given the "cold turkey" treatment (withdrawal without medication). Older ex-drug addicts help those who go through the stage of withdrawal with encouraging words, massage, and "tender loving care."

The Synanon method depends upon a kind of group therapy. Residents do house chores and engage in group therapy sessions. Every man and woman in Synanon is assigned a job: in the kitchen, in the office, on the house-maintenance gang, or on the "hustling crews" which canvass nearby business communities for contributions of food and services. Synanon operates gas stations in Santa Monica and San Diego. It has also gone into the engraving, storage pallet, and pen-and-pencil business. Profits are being used to defray expenses. It also owns several warehouses where its supplies are stored.

Membership is divided roughly into three groups, which represent stages of progress. Stage 1 is composed of those who live and work inside the house; stage 2, those who have jobs outside but still live in the house; stage 3, those who have graduated to living and working outside. Because of the Spartan life and rigid discipline, about 40 percent leave Synanon houses.

A number of books have been written about Synanon. (See Daniel H. Casriel, *So Fair a House;* Lewis Yablonsky, *The Tunnel Back.*) One of the most recent is by a nun, Barbara Leslie Austin, who along with another sister nun voluntarily joined the Synanon community for a summer to teach the children of drug addicts who were taking part in the community's rehabilitation program. The book is a graphic and detailed report on the whole Synanon program.[2] In addition to these books, a movie entitled *Synanon* has been released.

Daytop Village is another type of halfway house. There are three of these in the New York City area: Daytop Village at West Fourteenth Street, New York City, Daytop Lodge, and Daytop Village on Staten Island. They are sponsored by private funds and a grant from the National Institute of Mental Health. Daytop is an offshoot of Synanon and uses some of its techniques.

Daytop Village in New York City houses about one hundred addicts, ten of whom are women. Their ages range from sixteen to twenty-five years. Addicts come voluntarily or are paroled to Daytop on the orders of a judge. Volunteers may leave at any time, but the program is planned around an eighteen-month stay. Treatment consists of group therapy, working at household chores, educational seminars, and vocational training. Only two rules prevail: no violence and no chemicals. The director of Daytop claims that 85 percent remain clean.

All applicants are screened by older members who are ex-addicts. Candidates are confronted with seven co-ordinators, residents who have climbed the house's ladder of job promotion to roles of major responsibility. If accepted, the addict gets cold turkey. When the addict can overcome temptations at this "street level," he gets a job in S.P.A.N. (Special Projects Against Narcotics) Center in Greater New York.

The Daytop Theatre Company presents a rather successful play entitled *The Concept*. The cast consists of ex-addicts, and the production of *The Concept* is an outgrowth of Daytop's positive attitude toward life. None of the actors is professional, and the group as a whole has completed twelve drug-free years at Daytop. The idea of *The Concept* originated in October, 1966. It grew out of several months in workshop rehearsals and from constant discussion and sharing of ideas. Each scene was improvised, improved upon, recorded, until the present script was created.

The basic philosophy of Daytop is reflected in *The Concept*. It is summarized as follows:

We are here because there is no refuge, finally, from ourselves. Until a person confronts himself in the eyes and hearts of others, he is running. Until he suffers them to share his secret, he has no safety from it. Afraid to be known, he can know neither himself nor any other; he will be alone.

Where else but in our common ground can we find such a mirror? Here, together, a person can at last appear clearly to himself, not as the giant of his dreams nor the dwarf of his fears, but as a man, part of the whole, with his share in its purpose. In this ground we can each take root and grow, not alone anymore, as in death, but alive . . . to ourselves and others.[3]

One of the most effective and elaborate antidrug programs is operated by New York City's Human Resources Administration Addiction Services Agency. Initiated in 1966 by Mayor John Lindsay, the program in 1970 consisted of over fifty facilities with a staff of over four hundred. Through Phoenix Houses, neighborhood community centers, youth centers, "relatives of addicts" groups, and "aware citizens" groups, programs of prevention and treatment are carried on.

Only the Phoenix House program can be described in this study.[4] At present there are fourteen of these houses (called Phoenix from Egyptian mythology, which relates the story of a bird that consumed itself by fire and arose renewed from its ashes). Most of these houses are in poor neighborhoods where they are kept freshly painted and look as if they have sprung out of the ashes of the slums.

Each resident of a Phoenix House has a specific task

assignment, and participates in therapy or encounter sessions where the addict learns about himself and how he affects others. In seminars, scheduled and unscheduled subjects are discussed: world affairs, philosophy, or anything the youths want to talk about. All have to contribute, because this makes the individual feel that he is a part of the group. In this environment, the addict may find himself and live clean. As one Phoenix House director points out: "An addict is a person with a piece of personality missing. Like a jigsaw puzzle, Phoenix House helps him find the piece and put himself back together again." [5]

The educational program of Phoenix House stresses moral values, discipline, and responsibility. As one director declares: "Curing people is our meager accomplishment. Plugging a person into real values is what's important." [6] "Square" values are stressed because leaders of Phoenix House believe that, at heart, every addict is a square and wants to belong to the square society. Phoenix House helps its graduates to find outside employment and to live in the community. However, they may return to the House at any time for encounter sessions. A few remain in the program as leaders.

Matrix House, Inc., in Louisville, Kentucky, is another halfway house. It treats about twenty-five addicts at a time, helping them to bridge the gap between a narcotics hospital or other treatment facilities and society. This organization is designed to aid those who have shaken the physical habit of drugs, but need support to keep off of them. Ex-addicts interview all applicants, accepting or rejecting them.

At Matrix House, the treatment period is eighteen

months. For the first six to nine months, a resident spends all of his time in the house, helping perform household chores. In addition to doing menial jobs in the house, the ex-addict participates in an educational program designed to prepare him further to cope with the outside world. After this period, the ex-addict may spend another nine months or so living at the house at night, but working outside during the day.

Establishing drug abuse centers and halfway houses to treat addicts poses a dilemma. The problem is how to set up these facilities to solve a problem considered to be a crime without involving the police, who are responsible for suppressing the crime. The narcotics laws are on the books, and the police are responsible for enforcing them. Some working relationship between the centers and the law enforcement officers must be established. Unless drug abusers have some assurance of immunity from harassment and investigation by narcotics officers, they will probably shun the centers.

The public school can play a significant role in coping with the drug crisis. Perhaps the eventual success in controlling drug abuse is a sound educational program at every grade level. "Bits and pieces" programs in terms of talks and lectures in occasional general assemblies will not be adequate. Such programs are out of date and boring to most students. Drug education should start in the primary grades. Already at this early age, children are interested in talking about drugs. Of course, each program must be tailored to meet the needs of a specific group. Generally the teacher can discuss medicine and its effects on the body. The aim should be to develop a respect for the body and ways of keeping it healthy. At the junior and senior high school levels the curriculum should be more specific and the whole problem of drugs presented in detail.

Some states have already begun programs of drug education in the elementary, junior high, and senior high schools. In Texas, for example, every student in grades five through twelve will be required in 1970 to study drugs and drug abuse. The Texas legislature has directed the Texas Education Agency to develop curricula and teaching materials for the studies which will begin September 1, 1970.

Drug instruction should not be a separate discipline, but integrated into the whole curriculum. It should pervade other disciplines such as science, civics, sociology, political science, history, psychology, and courses on physical and mental health. Great care must be taken in planning a comprehensive and relevant program on drug abuse for the entire school. Facts about drugs must be honestly presented. Accurate information about the nature of drugs, their physiological and psychological effects, and therapeutic means of helping the drug dependent should be explored. Students at the high school level are sophisticated about drugs. "Scare" techniques will only turn them off. The American Psychiatric Association's Committee on Academic Freedom (December, 1969) sums up the proper approach:

Manifestly it is not enough to exhort that drug use is bad. Young people look to their peers and detect few ill effects. They witness their parents using cigarettes and alcohol despite knowledge of their ill effects. Educational efforts are essential—efforts that do not overstate the dangers but rather attempt to spell out what is and is not known. More research is essential and such research must not be hampered by inadequate funding, by ambiguity between federal and local guidelines, and by lack of availability of standard forms of drugs, as is so often the case presently.[7]

The American Psychiatric Association presents as its model of a comprehensive drug education program these essentials: (1) that educational programs on drug use be made available for children starting in the primary grades with the collaboration of physicians and other informed persons; (2) the development of educational materials appropriate to every grade level; (3) that support be given to research in drug use; (4) that counseling be made available in school systems to parents, youngsters, and educators, with the participation of psychiatrists and physicians; (5) that professional groups conduct training programs to bring their members up to date on knowledge of drugs; (6) that the curriculum of medical schools include information to prepare physicians to be helpful in clinical and educational settings; (7) that the American Psychiatric Association district branches collaborate with state councils of the American Medical Association in community and educational efforts with reference to the distribution of effective utilization of the American Medical Association's educational materials.[8]

Teachers, in order to converse effectively with students about drugs, must have certain qualities and qualifications. Among the essential qualities are: warmth of personality, ability to communicate well, sincere concern for students, personal authenticity, and the capacity to work with others and with agencies. Teachers can be prepared to deal with drug education by participating in in-service training programs. Courses dealing with drugs and drug abuse at the college level could be taken by teachers during the regular session or in summer school. The teacher is more of a neutral person than the parent and may counsel or refer the drug abuser to the school psychologist or psychiatrist. Once the teacher gets to know why the student is on drugs, he may be able to provide nondrug alternatives. The teacher may be the first to spot a drug pusher or proselytizer in the student body. By quickly dealing with these persons, he can prevent an epidemic of drug abuse in the school.

Teachers and students can plan together creative ways of attacking the drug problem in their school and nation. Let the students find out what laws exist in their state and community regarding the possession and sale of illegal drugs. Some could investigate the etiology or motivation for drug abuse among students. Others could report on the extent of drug abuse in their city, and the rehabilitation resources, or put on a sociodrama relating to the drug problem.

Administrators of public schools should be cognizant of the problem of drug abuse and take the initiative in developing a drug education program, providing the finances and facilities to put it into operation and maintain it. Practical actions, such as keeping the grounds clear of students who may take drugs in their parked cars, providing night classes for parents concerned about drug abuse, and working closely with such constructive forces as the PTA, drug abuse centers, doctors and hospitals, should be taken by principals and their staff.

There are other drug abuse rehabilitation programs in operation in this country. More are in the making. Public school officials and teachers must see that information about drugs is a part of the educational process and develop relevant curricula and employ competent persons to do the job. Every citizen should become acquainted with these resources in his own community. Then he will know where to turn for help.

CHAPTER 7

DRUGS AND RELIGIOUS EXPERIENCE

I take LSD primarily for the religious experience I get. Before I dropped acid I was an atheist. Now I believe in God. (*High school student.*)

A class of seminarians who heard this claim by a high school student were skeptical. Some thought it was sacrilegious. Such are the reactions of most people when the claim is made that there is some connection between psychedelic drugs and religious experience. Yet increasingly, many responsible persons, including professionals such as doctors, scientists, professors, and ministers, claim that there is a linkage between psychedelic tripping and authentic mystical experience. For them, religious experiences produced by drugs are no more artificial than those achieved by meditation, fasting, and organ music.

This chapter describes the nature of mysticism, proponents of psychedelic religion, and some current psychedelic churches. The following chapter presents a critical evaluation of the religious drug movement.

1. The Meaning of Mysticism

Mysticism, like religion, is one of the least precise terms in the English language. Dean Inge lists twenty-

six different efforts by as many authors to define it.[1]
Generally it is defined as an immediate awareness of
oneness of the self with God or the Ultimate. Religion
is man's relationship to God or to that which is experienced as the "ultimately real." Religion, to use Paul
Tillich's phrase, is "ultimate concern." Mysticism, in
which the soul becomes one with God, is the ultimate
concern of the religious person. Hence, mysticism is the
religious life at its very heart. In other words, mysticism
is the essence of religion, its most concentrated form. As
William James, the Harvard philosopher, declared, "Personal religious experience has its roots and centre in the
mystical states of consciousness." [2]

Religious experience at its highest occurs, then, when
the self encounters ultimate Being with the consequence
of a sense of unity which is defined as "mysticism."
There are, of course, different degrees of mystical experience along with numerous types of mysticism. All of
this makes it exceedingly difficult to arrive at any precise-
ness about the nature of religion and mysticism. But
both appear to be parts of the same package.

What constitutes a valid mystical experience? After a
thorough study of the literature on mysticism, W. T.
Stace isolated two types: extrovertive and introvertive.
He holds that the "universal core" of introvertive mysticism can be identified by seven criteria. They are: (1)
unitary consciousness, or a sense of cosmic oneness; (2)
transcendence of the spatial and temporal; (3) a sense
of objectivity or reality; (4) a sense of blessedness, joy,
peace; (5) a feeling that what is apprehended is sacred or
divine; (6) paradoxicality, or the experience of an identity
of opposites, which makes sense; and (7) alleged ineffa-
bility, or the inability of the mystic to verbalize his ex-

perience. Extrovertive mystical experience differs from the introvertive only in the first two characteristics in that it has no unitary consciousness, only a unifying vision "expressed abstractly by the formula 'All is One' perceived through the physical senses in numerous objects. In the case of the second criterion, the transcendence of time and space has no place in the extrovertive type." [3]

Psychedelic drug users claim to have a "central experience" of mystical religion which corresponds roughly with Stace's criteria of mysticism. Indeed, some persons claim that it is impossible to distinguish between the core experience of traditional mysticism and the central experience produced by psychedelics.

2. THE HIGH PRIEST OF THE DRUG CULT AND HIS ACOLYTES

Timothy Leary, formerly a psychology lecturer at Harvard, is the undisputed high priest of the chemical cult.[4] In the summer of 1960 in Mexico he ate seven "sacred mushrooms," and for the next five hours went through what he called "the deepest religious experience of my life." [5]

After this illumination or "profound transcendent experience," Leary was a changed man with a changed life. Since then he has devoted all his energies to trying to evangelize others. Returning to Harvard in the fall of 1960, he won his first convert, Dr. Richard Alpert, assistant director of Harvard's laboratory of human development. Together they experimented with psilocybin on psychology students. In 1961, Leary and Alpert set up a two-year pilot project involving thirty-five prisoners at the Massachusetts Correctional Institute at Concord. Its purpose was to determine whether or not psilocybin could keep repeaters of crime out of prison once they were freed. Results? Dr. Leary claimed that only 32 percent returned to prison after their release (67 percent is the national average).

Sidney Cohen notes that the analysis of what was actually done in the Leary experiment with the prisoners makes it less impressive. The follow-up period was too brief; the psilocybin takers enjoyed a special status in prison, a close friendly relation to the investigators, a parole course of instruction, assistance in securing employment and housing, and they maintained contacts with Leary and other friends at Harvard. The point is that none of these benefits were afforded the prisoners who were used for comparison.[6]

Harvard officials became concerned about Leary's experiments, especially those with students. Word leaked out that Leary and Alpert were advocating free use of hallucinogens and urging students to try them for themselves. Officials warned students not to become involved in drugs. Leary and Alpert moved their drug operations off campus near Boston. LSD usage was developing into an underground movement, with Leary as the chief priest. Leary and Alpert organized the movement into the International Foundation for Internal Freedom (IFIF).

In 1963 both Leary and Alpert were dismissed from their teaching positions at Harvard. Leary went to Mexico to set up new IFIF headquarters, but in six weeks the Mexican Government ordered him and his followers out of the country on the grounds that they were tourists engaged in unauthorized activities. After Leary was expelled from Mexico, IFIF folded, and he promptly founded the Castalia Foundation on an estate in Millbrook, New York, rented from William Hitchcock, a wealthy banker and a supporter of Leary.[7] Meantime, Alpert continued his campaign for legislation to permit responsible adults to take LSD for religious experience.

By 1964, Leary announced that the religious experience could be had without drugs through meditation, stroboscopic lights, and psychedelic music. But publicity about LSD resulted in the spread of experimentation through the colleges across the country. Leary was arrested in 1966 and charged with smuggling marijuana into this country from Mexico. Later he was arrested again at the Millbrook estate for the possession of marijuana. At the present time he is alleged to be in Algeria.

So much for Timothy Leary's career. Something must be said about his basic religious philosophy. Born and raised a Catholic, Leary became a prophet of psychedelic religion after ingesting mushrooms. He thinks that few people know what religious experience really is. For him, it is "the ecstatic, uncontrovertibly certain, subjective discovery of answers to four basic spiritual questions." [8] On the basis of his own experience and the hundreds of reports by the subjects he has "turned on," Leary advances the hypothesis that "those aspects of the psychedelic experience which subjects report to be ineffable and ecstatically religious involve a direct awareness of the process which physicists and biochemists and neurologists measure." [9] In other words, Leary holds that the data derived from drug sessions provide psychedelic correlates similar to modern scientific thinking with reference to questions about: (1) ultimate power; (2) life; (3) human destiny; and (4) the ego. Anyone, says Leary, who achieves this sort of data during a trip has an authentic religious experience, for psychedelic experience corresponds to scientific discoveries.

Leary claims that psychedelic reports correlate with the ultimate-power question, which seems to describe the mysterious and complex origin and development of the universe. Subjects speak of merging with pure energy and white light, the awareness that everything is a dance of particles, of world-ending explosions, of the cyclical nature of creation and dissolution. These reports correlate with the scientific answer to the life question in terms of participation in cellular flow, of being a one-celled organism floating down arterial waterways, and visions of microscopic processes. Also, these reports correlate with the scientific answer to the human-destiny question when the LSD subjects experience early forms of subhuman species evolution as their cortical cells "remember" back along an unbroken chain of electrical transformations that connect every person back to "the original thunderbolt in the per-Cambrian mud." [10]

Finally, psychedelic trippers report correlations with the scientific answer to the ego question. The biochemical neurologist, thinks Leary, is the man "who can locate 'you' in the five-billion-year sequence by describing the capacities of your cortex. Your consciousness is a biochemical electrical process." [11] For Leary, the psychedelic answer to the ego question is the crux of the LSD experience. When the subject's cortex is turned on, he discovers who he is from his ten-billion-cell cerebral computer and the relation of his ego to the total energy field. This knowledge produces in the subject a sense of awe, humility, and reverence.

The question arises as to whether these biochemical

visions are in fact religious. Leary thinks so. The "Divine Process" presents itself in many ways. It produced the substance called LSD, which is the "Key," an organic molecule, "to this direct visionary world." [12]

Another advocate of the use of LSD for religious experience is Walter Pahnke, M.D., who has conducted numerous experiments with psychedelic drugs. Psychedelic experiences vary, he says, with dosage and the range of tolerance in the user. These experiences are divided into five types: psychotic, psychodynamic, cognitive, aesthetic, and psychedelic peak (transcendental or mystical). The latter category has to do with the mystical experience derived from drugs. From his studies of cases of mystical experience, classical and contemporary, Pahnke has worked out certain criteria of religious experience. Drawing upon W. T. Stace's categories in *Mysticism and Philosophy,* he accepts Stace's seven characteristics of mystical experience and adds two more: transiency of the psychedelic peaks and positive changes in attitudes and behavior toward the subject's self and others.[13]

As a part of his doctoral study at Harvard, Pahnke worked out an experiment to secure evidence that psychedelic chemicals do release profound religious experiences. In the setting of a Good Friday service, ten Protestant theological students were administered 30 milligrams of psilocybin and ten other students a semiplacebo. The drug was given "double blind," which means that neither Dr. Pahnke nor his subjects knew which ten were ingesting psilocybin and which ten the placebo that made up the control group.

Written data from the subjects were submitted to three judges, who, without being informed about the nature of the study, were asked to judge the data in the light of nine criteria of the "universal core" of mystical experience. The results revealed that those who received the psilocybin had an experience indistinguishable from the criteria defined by the elements of a mystical experience.[14]

Subsequent experiments convinced Dr. Pahnke that psychedelic drugs can trigger mystical experience. He calls for further research under supervision for maximal safety. He suggests two areas of future psychedelic research. First, with terminal cancer patients because the experience of death has a crucial place in almost all religions. Secondly, he thinks that psychedelic therapy may have a role to play to make life more livable for terminal patients. The use of psychedelics reduces fear, anxiety, and apprehension in some cases. Pilot projects in this area already appear to be a promising approach in helping to ease the agony and isolation of death.[15]

Walter Houston Clark, professor emeritus of psychology of religion at Andover Newton Theological Seminary in Newton Centre, Massachusetts, is also convinced that psychedelic drugs can and do trigger genuine religious experience. He has studied the problem for several years, attended seminars organized by Dr. Timothy Leary at Harvard, and has helped to guide numerous administrations of psilocybin and LSD to subjects. He himself has tried LSD and psilocybin several times. He thinks that drugs prove the most ready access to what William James declared to be the root of religion, namely, mystical experience.[16] So convinced is he of the significance of psychedelic drugs for religious experience that he thinks that the discovery of LSD "might" rank with the Copernican revolution.[17] For him, psychedelic drugs are potentially useful tools for the study of religious experience and mental health therapy. The churches, he thinks, must not ignore this potential use.

Clark calls for the responsible use of psychedelics. Even under controlled conditions, he admits, one must frankly face dangers. Persons who have suicidal tendencies should not take the drug, nor should pregnant women use it. Yet psychedelic experience, he thinks, is relatively safe. The fact that it is not always safe requires the user to take a calculated risk. Besides the psychological hazards of the drugs, there are also possibilities of physical harm that cannot be neglected. But he concludes that drug-induced mysticism is an expression of grace in modern form.[18] Besides, he asserts, great religious figures have never been afraid of risks.

With reference to laws relating to drugs, Clark suggests the following: (1) that psychedelics be distinguished from the addictive drugs; (2) that care be taken to avoid trying to scare young people by telling them only the dangers of drugs; (3) that all laws for possession of psychedelic drugs (as distinct from the sale) be repealed; (4) that government-sponsored and licensed psychedelic clinics staffed with experts be established where people who wish to take psychedelic drugs for any reason may apply; (5) that the government provide licensing for specially trained psychiatrists and psychologists to use the psychedelic drugs in their practice and research; and (6) that permission be given to religious institutions to use the drugs in worship.[19]

From the background of a lifelong interest in religious experience and many years of research and extensive study of the religious properties of the psychedelic chemicals, Clark describes the need for continuing research in the drug field, the need for more scientists to ingest drugs so that they can deal factually with their effects, the necessity for the church to be open to the use of psychedelics, and the need for small enclaves of worshipers to meet in their homes and to experiment with drugs. "If such adventurers on the frontiers of spirituality," says Clark, "who still keep in touch with their primary religious institutions, can demonstrate the soundness of their methods, then perhaps they may some day be allowed to enrich timid churches through a new and vital strain." [20]

3. PSYCHEDELIC CHURCHES

At present psychedelic churches are emerging outside the religious establishments. Several of these churches have already been founded by persons who are convinced that psychedelic drugs can play an important role in religious experience. Among them are the Native American Church, the Church of the Awakening, the Neo-American Church, and the League for Spiritual Discovery.

The Native American Church, composed of approximately two hundred and fifty thousand members made up of Indian tribes, is one of the most visible psychedelic churches today.[21] A federation of North American Indians, the members use peyote primarily in religious experience. The church claims that it is Christian, and that its moral teachings of family responsibility, hard work, love of one another, and abstinence from alcohol does not depart markedly from the teachings of the typical American middle-class Christian churches.[22]

Members of a local Native American Church hold

their meetings in an enclosure from sundown on Saturday to sunrise on Sunday. Dressed in their best clothing, members gather for the expressed purpose of worship. Each adult may take four peyote buttons to chew (sometimes buttons are boiled in water to make a tea). During the service, they may have as many as four more buttons. By Sunday morning the effect of the peyote disappears, without apparent aftereffects. After a Sunday morning breakfast, the Indians return to their homes.

For years the peyote Indians have been opposed to the use of the drug by both nonmembers of their own people and whites. Some have been brought into the courts and imprisoned for violating drug laws. However, in most cases when the laws governing the religious use of peyote have been tested in the courts, they have been overturned. In a 1964 decision based on the First Amendment of the Bill of Rights, the California Supreme Court ruled that Indian members of the Native American Church could not be legally deprived of peyote used in their religious ceremonies. The court explained that the sacramental use of peyote "composes the cornerstone" of their religion. Indeed, the court pointed out that peyote used in the Indians' services is more than a sacrament, since prayers are directed to it much as they are to the Holy Spirit. The court concluded: "To forbid the use of peyote is to remove the theological heart of Peyotism." [23]

The decision of the California Supreme Court to permit the use of peyote in religious worship poses the question whether other drugs such as LSD can be used in religious experience. No doubt the issue will, sooner or later, be tested in the courts.

The Church of the Awakening was incorporated as a

religious institution in 1963 by John and Louisa Aiken, retired physicians. Located in Socorro, New Mexico, it has about three hundred and fifty members. Membership may also be held in other religious bodies. In a statement of purpose, the church defines religion in its inner meaning as "the search within one's own consciousness for the Self, which is Being, which is Life." [24] Its external function is expressed in terms of love, service, and growth. To aid in the search, the church administers the psychedelic sacrament or peyote. The church has not yet succeeded in its appeal to the Bureau of Narcotics and Dangerous Drugs of the Justice Department for permission to use peyote freely for religious experience.

The Church of the Awakening is identified by Braden as the middle-class right wing of the psychedelic church movement.[25] The composition of its membership is made up of businessmen and professional people. They claim that their religious lives have been made stronger and deeper because of their participation in the services using peyote. The use of the peyote sacrament is observed once every three months.

Arthur Kleps, a psychologist, founded the Neo-American Church in 1964. He calls himself Chief Boo-Hoo, the Patriarch of the East, a title that reminds him not to take himself too seriously. A membership of six hundred is claimed for his church. LSD is used as the sacrament of the Neo-American Church. One of the basic beliefs of the congregation is that the use of psychedelics for religious experience is a right of all citizens. Appearing before the Special Senate Judiciary Subcommittee on Narcotics in Washington in 1966, Klep declared that the religious use of psychedelic drugs is a right which the Constitution of the United States confers upon every citizen. At this same hearing Kleps made it clear that Timothy Leary was the patron saint of the Neo-American Church. "We regard . . . [Leary]," he said, "with the same special love and respect as was reserved by the early Christians for Jesus, by Muslims for Mohammed or the Buddhists for Gautama." [26]

The Neo-American Church, says Braden, represents the "bohemian left wing" of the drug cult. Its chief aim appears to be "the appreciation of Transcendental Reality." Though officially the church espouses a kind of "revolutionary nihilism," most of the members appear to be quietistic.[27] In other words, theirs is a strategy of withdrawal from the system, its goals and rewards.

The League of Spiritual Discovery became a legally incorporated religion by Timothy Leary in 1966. It is dedicated, as he says, "to the ancient sacred sequence of turning-on, tuning-in, and dropping-out. Its aim is to help re-create every man as a God and every woman as a Goddess." [28] The seal of the League is a mandala—the endless circle circumscribing a four-leaf lotus made by a double infinity sign.

In his book *High Priest,* Leary says that it is "the first of a four-volume biblical account of the birth, structural growth, exile, return, persecution, redemption, and flowering of the LSD religious cult." [29] The account of Trip 1 begins with a paraphrase of Gen. 1:1–2 and John 1:1–2:

In the beginning was the Turn On. The flash, the illumination. The electric trip. The sudden bolt of energy that starts the new system. The Turn On was God. All things were made from the Turn On and without Him was not any thing made. In this Turn On was life; and the life was the light of men.[30]

The story of the Creation and the Fall in Genesis is interpreted in psychedelic terms and images. On a psychedelic trip, the subject encounters the great Turn On, the Light which shines in the darkness and cannot be put out. When one turns on, the bolt shatters structure and there is nothing but energy ($E = MC^2$), which lights every man who comes into the world. Man is a two-billion-year-old carrier of Light and born of the Light that flashed in the pre-Cambrian mud, the Light that made flesh.[31]

To tune in is to bear witness of the Light so that all men may believe. In this experience one's illusions are shattered and the body is a temple of the Light, and the subject begins to build a structure to preserve and glorify the Light.

To tune in one must drop out, that is, detach oneself from the fake-prop studio of the empire game and do nothing but guard and glorify the Light.[32]

Thus Leary's categories of turn on, tune in, and drop out have deeper significance than is popularly realized. One senses that he takes his theory with deep seriousness and proclaims it with evangelistic passion. As high priest of his church, Leary has led in the psychedelic celebrations performed in some of the major cities throughout the nation. The central theme of his sermons has been "turn on, tune in, and drop out." By this latter injunction, as has been noted, Leary does not mean the complete withdrawal from the world, but from the round of meaningless activities of the straight society. This is necessary in order to spend a maximum of time in spiritual exploration, which he thinks is the *raison d'être* for living.

The bible of the League for Spiritual Discovery is the *Psychedelic Review,* founded by Leary and a colleague, Gunther Weil, who also served as its first editors. Leary's psychedelic prayers have been published and they reveal his mystical nature and poetic insights.[33] Generally, Leary expresses his religious beliefs in Eastern religious terminology. He thinks that there are basic differences between the religious experience of the Eastern religions and those of the West. He is closer to the pantheistic God of the East than to the transcendent God of the West. In his view, the LSD experience supports the Eastern and not the Western God.[34]

CHAPTER 8

PSYCHEDELIC RELIGION:
FACT OR FANTASY

Do PSYCHEDELICS really duplicate genuine, nondrug religious and mystical experience? Does the "experience" reveal anything about God? On the basis of numerous studies and experiments, one is forced to concede that drugs do produce some sort of religious experience. There are too many testimonies to this effect to reject totally this assumption. Phenomenologically, psychedelics do appear to produce some of the characteristics of mystical experience established by W. T. Stace and Walter Pahnke. But there is considerable debate as to whether the religious experience produced by psychedelic drugs is valid and genuine.

For one thing, psychedelic religious experience is highly subjective. Charles Baudelaire, the hashish-eating poet, declares that all the drug does is to magnify the natural and merely to reflect the thoughts and fancies of a dreamer. It is like a magnifying mirror and all that a user sees is an enlarged image of himself. In short, hashish reveals to the taker "nothing except himself." [1] Another thing appears to be clear: psychedelic drugs only trigger, release, or serve as catalysts of religious experience. They cannot produce anything that is not already in the subject. Walter Clark stresses this fact, though he thinks that drugs may, in a sense, be a part of a complex of factors in the "mystery-producing" encounter with ultimate reality. He illustrates the point:

Just as photographic chemicals bring to light the picture already imprinted on the film, the psychedelic chemicals have, in actual practice, introduced many people to an appreciation for music, a capacity for art or a sensitivity to poetry that was there but which they never dreamed they had.[2]

Just so, thinks Clark, chemicals can deliver out of the depths of the self an awareness of the holy and a knowledge that the "stuff" which men are made of is also divine.

Of course, the psychedelic user will exclaim: "That is just the point. On drugs one does see nothing but himself. What else is there to see?" Therein lies the problem. When a man sees only himself, he tends to think that he is God, as Baudelaire has so clearly noted.[3] A high school student explained to a class of seminarians: "The religious experience on LSD which I have is not a feeling of being with God, but rather that I *am* God." He theorized: "God is nature and I am nature; therefore I must be God." Here the self is exaggerated and magnified to the level of God himself. The logic is irrefutable. But if there is any validity in the Christian Biblical revelation, man is not God, but made in the *imago Dei*, the image of God. Man's own nature should convince him of his finitude and egocentricity. One suspects that, once off drugs, he who boasts of being God will freely admit his own imperfections and confess to his lack of omnipotence and omniscience unless, of course, he is dreaming.

The drug user will argue that his religious experience is no more subjective than that of the theologian. If his experience cannot be verified by empirical demonstration, neither can the theologian's. But there are differences in the experiences when the simple Scriptural test, "You will know them by their fruits," is applied. Psychedelic theophanies lack staying power. As Huston Smith observes, there is reason for doubting "the carryover" of psychedelic experiences into everyday existence.[4] When the LSD user comes down from his high, his vision of God is gone and "he finds himself," as Swami Prabhavananda says, "spiritually dry, and empty. . . . God is as distant as ever."[5]

Moreover, psychedelic drugs do not produce the quality of transformation that the encounter with the Christian God in Christ does. This calls for a lifelong commitment and pilgrimage under the Lordship of Christ. Such an experience cannot be produced by ingesting a drug or turned off when the effects of a drug dies down. Besides, many who continue to use drugs deteriorate psychologically and emotionally, and it is difficult to see how this could be a part of real religious experience.

The psychedelic religion does not pass the ethical test. Allegedly, psychedelics engender feelings of universal love, brotherhood, and tolerance. Here again, the test is not words but deeds. In their brilliant and comprehensive study of the varieties of psychedelic experience, R. E. L. Masters and Jean Houston point out that in the 1950's prior to the development of love-oriented literature and the increasing popularity of brotherhood, the psychedelic experience rarely ever produced a sense of love and brotherhood.[6] Though drug users now claim these feelings, there is scant evidence that they are "more loving" in fact.

Based on case studies, Masters and Houston conclude that:

The claim of universal love and tolerance is not persuasive unless supported by appropriate actions. Since most often it is based upon some form of self-deception; and since the need to experience a cosmic benevolence seems satisfied by words without deeds, we do not encounter the appropriate actions very often. In the case of the drug subject this particular self-deception rather often arises out of a kind of narcissistic solipsism in which the person regards the world as existing in himself or for-himself. Then, what the subject loves, in fact, *is* himself.[7]

Another ethical weakness of the psychedelic faith is that it tends toward an ingroupishness. What feelings of love, brotherhood, and tolerance the drug users possess are expressed largely to brothers on drugs. The psychedelic experience becomes a badge of belonging to a group apart from others.[8] They tend to cut themselves off from others, the squares, and withdraw into "a tight little microcosm of fellow true believers." [9]

Instant love, which psychedelic ingesters never take the pains to define, cannot be achieved by merely swallowing a pill or smoking pot. It too often happens that instant love instantly disappears when the effects of the drug subside. Usually when the user comes down from a drug-induced feeling of lovingness and faces a concrete neighbor, his "galloping agape" subsides "to the usual trot with occasional prances." [10]

As for the general deteriorating moral effects of drugs

on the user, Baudelaire has provided a gruesome picture. Specifically he notes that the will is a special victim. Drugs stultify the will, making it difficult to act responsibly toward oneself and others. He points to the disastrous consequences of a nation whose citizens, legislators, and soldiers might be intoxicated with drugs.[11]

The psychedelic religion also fails the social test. Huston Smith has perceptibly observed that this movement lacks a social philosophy for relating itself to society, that it is antinomian, and that it leaves nothing exoteric.[12] The movement tends to withdraw, "drop out" of society, rather than remain in it to redeem it. There are reasons for this, namely, that the movement has no apocalyptic expectation, no revolutionary blueprint, and no utopian hope.[13] Its antinomian posture ignores the need for man to be restrained by moral forces and law. And the movement tends to blur "the distinction between what in religion is properly esoteric and exoteric."[14] That is to say, to claim that there are secrets in religion which are only for the privileged is to deny these to some on the grounds that they are not capable of receiving them. The drug movement is an esoteric cult. Dr. Sidney Cohen, chief of the psychosomatic service at Wadsworth Veterans Administration Hospital in Los Angeles, notes that there is a large segment of people who should never take LSD and for them to do so would have disastrous results.[15]

Genuine mysticism is characterized by a balance between contemplation and ethical action. Meister Eckhart, the medieval mystic, declared that:

What a man takes in contemplation he must pour out in love. If a man was in rapture such as St. Paul experienced, and if he knew a person who needed something of him, I think it would be far better out of love to leave the rapture and serve the needy man. It is better to feed the hungry than to see even such visions as St. Paul saw.[16]

The drug cult tends toward insularity and toward placing its greatest interest in the experience at the cost of ethics. Like so many so-called mystics, the psychedelic religious splashes in the bath of delicious emotions and weird visions. Theirs is an escape from life and from the hard work that must be done in the world to humanize it.

Psychedelic religion, especially that of Leary, makes dubious claims about providing the same answers to life's mysteries and problems that science does. In response to Leary's theory of psychedelic correlates to scientific answers to the ultimate-power, life, human-destiny, and ego questions, Dr. William Hordern notes that Leary blurs the distinction between religion and science. Leary claims that science answers questions in terms of objective, observed, public data and religion answers the same questions in terms of direct incontrovertible personal experience. Hordern observes that science and religion differ not only in "the method in which they answer questions, but in the nature of the questions they ask." [17] Religion asks, Who? not, How? as does science. As for the life question, science asks what the factors were which led to life, while the religious question is, What is the meaning of life? These are questions which science can neither ask nor answer.

Hordern goes on to point out that Biblical faith is opposed to religion per se, that is, the attempt to find God in natural objects. Rather, God is known, at least for the Christian, not by looking at nature or into himself, but by hearing God's message in Jesus Christ.[18]

Mysticism tends to move toward pantheism. So does the psychedelic mystical experience. Pantheism is the theory that God is everything and everything is God. In this doctrine the transcendence of God is lost. God becomes completely immanent in all things. (Such a view makes God a captive of his own creation.) Hence, when the drug user sees God as nature and himself as a part of nature, he concludes he is God. This accounts for the sense of omnipotence and the illusion of omnicompetence.

Psychedelics tend to produce an aesthetic and not the authentic religious experience. Pahnke concedes that most subjects experimenting with psychedelics attain only the aesthetic level.[19] Perhaps many of the users of psychoactive drugs reach only the level of what Søren Kierkegaard calls the aesthetic stage of life which recognizes no binding universals and seizes what pleasure and meaning it can from day to day. This is the stage which must pass through the ethical or transitional stage to the religious.[20]

Although the exponents of the psychedelic faith concede that the proper setting and state of mind are essential to a religious trip, it is an instant way of achieving illumination and mystical experience. This is diametrically different from nondrug or traditional mysticism in which the experience is achieved by a long and disciplined process of prayer, meditation, fasting, and devotions.

There is a question whether instant grace or mystico-religious experience can be had without disciplined spiritual exercises. Even so it cannot possibly produce the kind of high character that is achieved in the struggle for the experience. Sidney Cohen illustrates the difference:

The difference between the "easy" and the "hard" ways must be similar to the situation in which one man climbs the Zugspitze and another takes the ski-lift. The view from the top is the same for both. The mountain climber has sweated and striven against dangers. His view must be different from the ski-lift rider's because it incorporates the struggle and the triumph. Ski-lift transcendence can approach that of the mountain climber's only if the prior life preparation has also been one of training and self-discipline.[21]

Herein lies a basic difference between the drug-induced and the traditional mystical experience. There is simply no supersonic flight to the Celestial City without preparation in terms of discipline and training. This is true not only in Eastern religions, but also in the Judeo-Christian religion. Genuine mystical experience "can be obtained only by a journey on foot by way of the Slough of Despond, the Hill of Difficulty, Doubting Castle, and the rest." [22] The Christian life is a pilgrimage for which no pill can serve as a substitute. It involves struggle with principalities and powers, but in the battle the warrior achieves character, an increase of insight into himself, and awareness of the presence of God.

Granted that the psychedelic religious experience and the traditional or orthodox type reveal some significant parallels as measured by the seven-point typology established by W. T. Stace, the question remains as to where the source of the experience is. Does it stem from God or the fantasy of a super drug-charged cortex? Is its source in genuine mysticism or some other type?

Prof. R. C. Zaehner, a scholar of Eastern history and religion, holds that psychedelic religious experience falls short of the authentic type, which is ontologically different. His conclusions are based on (1) his own experience with psychedelics, which he describes as "utterly trivial"; (2) the experiences of others, which appear to be religious but are not authentically so because they stem from a kind of nature mysticism in which the self is united with the natural world or they are based on monistic mysticism in which the soul dissolves in the impersonal absolute. Authentic mysticism, Zaehner believes, is grounded in theistic mysticism in which the self encounters the living, personal God.[23]

One may argue, as do Masters and Houston, that the peyote rituals of the North American Indians produce theistic religious experiences.[24] But it must be kept in mind that these peyote users have a Christian orientation which is theistic to begin with. Peyote only intensifies and distorts the theism that they derive from the Biblical revelation. The experience reflects a syncretism of Christian teachings, folklore, and other data.

By now it must be clear that this writer rejects the claim that psychedelics produce authentic mysticoreligious experience. A recapitulation of reasons follows. The psychedelic mystical experience is too subjective, nebulous, kaleidoscopic. Mystical language is used, but the experience is different. It describes nature and monistic mysticism and not theistic. Authentic theism does not produce the confusion, whirling patterns, pain of being thrust into heaven and then into hell, paranoia, and the fear of going insane. The true mystic needs no expert guide to bring him down safely from the mystical peak.[25] He is not open to suggestibility, as in the case of the drug user. Ethical expression in the psychedelic mystical experience is weak and confined largely to the ingroup. In many cases, drugs have a deteriorating effect on moral behavior. One has only to reflect on the fading flower people called hippies of Haight-Ashbury or observe the behavior of youngsters on drugs in one's own neighborhood.[26]

There is the possibility that the drug-taker will end up with a bad trip. As Leary admits and is worried about, there is no way to predict where the tripper will go.[27] And the possibility of doing something irrational and dangerous following a drug session is always there. Leary's *High Priest* closes with a description of his driving after a drug session and having to struggle to resist the impulse to swerve the car with his wife and another occupant over a cliff.[28] Or take the case of his eighteen-year-old son who, after taking drugs, declared that he was "illuminated" and then burned a thousand-dollar bill because he saw money as a paper illusion.[29]

The crux of the problem of psychedelic religion is its source. It has no ontological underpinning. Rather, its source is within man himself. And this accounts for the dubious spiritual and ethical fruits of the experience. There is no question in the mind of the Christian as to the source of his religious experience. It is personal and existential commitment to the God, who in many and various ways,

spoke of old to our fathers by the prophets; but in these last days he has spoken to us by a Son, whom he appointed the heir of all things, through whom also he created the world. He reflects the glory of God and bears the very stamp of his nature, upholding the universe by his word of power (Heb. 1:1–3).

This God is personal, not pantheistic, and is apprehended not by chemicals but by commitment in terms of faith, repentance, confession of sins, and the living of life under his Lordship as revealed in Jesus Christ.

CHAPTER 9

THE BIBLE AND DRUGS

THE PROFESSION OF PHARMACY was well known in both Old and New Testament periods. Indeed, the art of the apothecary extends as far back as 3700 B.C., the date of the earliest known prescription.[1] The ancient Egyptians had over eight hundred prescriptions, which took the form of salves, plasters, poultices, snuffs, pills, fumigations, and suppositories.[2] The Babylonians also had numerous prescriptions, while the Assyrians had over five hundred derived from plants, minerals, and animals.[3]

1. DRUGS OF THE BIBLE

In comparison with surrounding nations, the pharmacopoeia of the Hebrews seems scant indeed. Not one Hebrew is actually mentioned in the Old Testament as being an apothecary. Hananiah, a man who helped to rebuild the walls of Jerusalem, is mentioned as the son of an apothecary, but he could have been a perfumer or mixer of ointments (Neh. 3:8; the King James Version says "apothecaries" and the Revised Standard Version "perfumers"). The Hebrew verb *rakach* means "to mix, to compound oil for ointment." Be that as it may, the large number of derivatives from this verb, all concerned with the perfumer or the pharmacist, indicate the extensive nature of this profession.[4]

No doubt the Hebrews acquired much of their knowledge of pharmacology from their exile experience in Egypt and their captivity in Babylon, along with contacts with other nations under the reign of Solomon. However, the Hebrews developed their own types of pharmacology and methods of prescribing and administering it.

Not all the drugs mentioned in the Bible and used among the Hebrews and early Christians can be dealt with in this chapter.[5] Among some of those commonly used was balm, an aromatic resin from the balsam tree. It was reputed to have medicinal and healing properties (Jer. 8:22). Jeremiah, the prophet, advises the taking of balm for pain and healing (Jer. 51:8). According to Kramer, there is an official balm of Gilead bud in contemporary medicine obtained in North America.[6]

The mandrake is a stemless herb with green rosette leaves and a divided fleshy root. It is related to the nightshade family of drug plants, as are belladonna, henbane, and jimsonweed. Described as a drug for pain, gallbladder trouble, insomnia, boils, and gout, it was also used as a purgative.[7] Hippocrates recognized its use to relieve depression and anxiety, while Aristotle classified it as a drug to induce slumber. Discorides was reputed to have used mandrake wine as an anesthetic when he was an army surgeon in the service of the emperor Nero.[8] A. G. Frazer notes that the drug was used in the Greek period for people about to undergo surgery.[9]

The mandrake's small fruit and fleshy root were also reputed to induce fertility. In Gen. 30:14–16, the story is told of how Reuben found mandrakes in a field and brought them to his mother, Leah, one of the wives of Jacob. Rachel, Jacob's favorite wife, still childless, asked for some of the mandrakes. In return, Rachel agreed to permit Jacob to lie with Leah, who conceived and bore a child. Rachel was not helped by the mandrakes and when she did bear a child, it was not due to the mandrakes but because "Yahweh remembered" Rachel (v. 22). Since the mandrake was a type of sedative, some writers think that Rachel desired it to ease her pain in childbirth.[10] But this theory may be discounted in the light of the fact that Rachel requested the mandrakes at the time of her sterility, not just prior to childbirth.

Gall is mentioned several times in the Scriptures (Deut. 29:18; Jer. 9:15; 23:15; Lam. 3:19; Amos 6:12; Matt. 27:34; Acts 8:23, etc.). It was a poisonous and bitter herb and a narcotic. The term is used frequently by the Biblical writers as a synonym for bitterness and tragedy. When used with the word "wormwood" it expressed the extremity of bitterness. Wormwood is mentioned in Deut. 29:18 and Jer. 23:15, and other places, and is found in the deserts of Palestine. It is a plant that has a bitter taste and was used as a folk medicine.

Myrrh comes from a low thorny shrub and produces a soft yellowish resin from its branches. The Hebrews used it for incense in their worship. Also, it was prized as a perfume and, mixed with other spices, as a preparation for anointing a body before burial. According to the historian Herodotus, myrrh was used as a salve for ulcers. In ancient Assyria it was used in suppositories, as a mouthwash, and as an ointment for the eyes and ears.[11] Myrrh was one of the three gifts of the Magi (Matt. 2:11). According to Mark, myrrhed wine was offered to Jesus just before he was crucified (Mark 15:23). It was also used to anoint his body before burial (John 19:39).

Hyssop is a perennial shrub one to two feet high, with white flowers. In Egypt the Hebrews took a bunch of hyssop dipped in blood and touched their doorposts with it during the Passover (Ex. 12:22). Survivors of the ancient Samaritan sect still use branches of hyssop for sprinkling the blood of the Passover sacrifice. Hyssop was also used in the purification of lepers and of diseased houses (Lev., ch. 14), and in the New Testament a sponge full of vinegar was put upon hyssop and held to the mouth of Jesus at his crucifixion (John 19:29).

Vinegar was procured from overfermented or soured grape wine (Num. 6:3) and by pouring water on leftover grape skins after the juice had been pressed out. In diluted form, vinegar was considered to be a refreshing drink. However, it increased one's thirst (Ps. 69:21). Nazirites were forbidden to drink vinegar because of its association with wine and strong drink (Num. 6:2–3).

Vinegar is mentioned in the New Testament only in relation to Christ's crucifixion (Matt. 27:48; Mark 15:36; Luke 23:36; John 19:29–30). Mark indicates that a drink of "myrrhed wine," an opiate, was offered to Jesus before he was placed on the cross (Mark 15:23) and vinegar later (v. 36). Matthew declares that it was wine "mingled with gall" which was offered to Jesus before being crucified, and that when Jesus was on the cross and cried, "My God, my God, why hast thou forsaken me?" someone, presumably a soldier, took a sponge filled with vinegar and put it on a reed and offered it to Jesus. Luke mentions only the vinegar that a soldier offered to Jesus after he was on the cross. John states that Jesus was on the cross when "vinegar on hyssop" was given to him.

What shall we make of all this? In the Marcan account

Jesus was offered a narcotic (myrrhed wine) to ease the pain of the crucifixion. It was the custom of the good women of Jerusalem, as an act of mercy, to provide an opiate for criminals condemned to death by crucifixion (*Talmud Babylonia*). Perhaps "the daughters of Jerusalem" who sorrowfully accompanied the procession to Calvary offered the drink to Jesus (Mark 15:23; Luke 23:28). In the Matthean account, the author changes "myrrhed wine" to "sour wine" or "vinegar mingled with gall" to fulfill the prophecy of Ps. 69:21. Luke indicates that while Jesus was on the cross, a Roman soldier offered him vinegar, either as an act of mercy or to increase his thirst and suffering. The latter seems more probable, for Roman soldiers were not given to acts of mercy during executions. John speaks of "vinegar on hyssop," perhaps offered as a symbol of the Passover ritual.

Although Jesus accepted the vinegar, he refused the myrrhed wine. In rejecting the anesthetic he greeted death with an unclouded mind and open eyes. Had he taken the opiate, he may not have uttered the gracious "sayings" from the cross. The example of Jesus' refusal to cloud his consciousness with a drug should be communicated to the drug user of today.

2. Drug Abuse in the Bible

There is no reference in the Bible to either the use or the abuse of hallucinogenic drugs such as peyote and cannabis, though these drugs were known centuries before Christ. However, attempts have been made to substantiate the use of psychoactive drugs by Biblical characters. For example, Dr. Mark D. Altschule, editor of a medical journal, claims that he has unraveled the truth of what actually happened to Adam and Eve in the Garden of Eden. The fruit that Eve ate contained a hallucinogen! He made this discovery in an old English poem called "Genesis B" (see *Speculum*, Vol. 44, No. 86, 1969). It describes how the serpent promised Eve that if she ate the fruit of the tree of knowledge, she would see heaven and the throne of God. After eating the fruit, she had a vision that she described in words of great joy. All things seemed brighter to her and she could see at great distances.

The poem indicates that Eve only *thought* she saw all these wonders. Meantime she had tempted Adam to eat the fruit, but he had no vision. When the effects of the drug diminished, both discovered they had been ruined.

Altschule concludes that the fruit must have been of the *Solanaceae* family, a variety of which grows as trees in warm climates and has berries containing hallucinogens of the scopolamine type. He concludes:

Regardless of which plant history proves to have led to Eve's hallucinogens in the Garden, the event is worthy of serious study. It foretold what today seems to be a frequent occurrence, the ruin of a young person by a friend, lover, or spouse who induced him or her to try a drug through the promise of a beautiful experience.[12]

The doctor appears seriously to believe the above account of what happened in the garden. His theory is bad theology, but the story does contain an excellent moral.

There is no doubt that wine was the most abused drug among Biblical people. The Hebrew prophets constantly inveighed against its immoderate use. Isaiah condemns those who "tarry late in the evening till wine inflames them" (ch. 5:11; cf. v. 22). He denounces priests and prophets who "reel" and "stagger" because of too much wine (ch. 28:7). Proverbs is replete with warnings against overindulgence in strong drink. Solomon asserts: "Wine is a mocker, strong drink a brawler; and whoever is led astray by it is not wise" (Prov. 20:1).

In the New Testament there is no absolute condemnation of wine as a beverage. It was commonly used at meals and weddings (John 2:1–11). Paul recommended that the young minister Timothy take a little wine for stomach trouble and other ailments (I Tim. 5:23). Wine was also commonly used in dressing wounds (Luke 10:34). However, the apostle Paul condemned excessive use of wine (Eph. 5:18). He insisted that leaders of the church, bishops and deacons, should not be drunkards. Furthermore, he declared that if drinking wine caused a weaker brother to stumble and to slip back into pagan ways, the Christian should not drink it (Rom. 14:13–21).

The Bible strongly condemns magicians, witches, and sorcerers, who used drugs in connection with their art. The Greek word for "sorcery" is *pharmakeia* (from which is derived the term "pharmacy") and literally means the act of administering drugs and then giving magical potions. It is derived from *pharmakon,* and from Homer on down means a drug. Paul refers to *pharmakeia* ("sorcery") and so does the author of Revelation (Gal. 5:20; Rev. 9:21). The practice included the use of incantations, magical acts, and drugs. In the Old Testament, *pharmakeia* is represented in the Hebrew term *kishsēph,* "a sorcerer" (Jer. 27:9; cf. Deut. 18:10; II Kings 21:6; II Chron. 33:6; Isa. 3:2). In the Septuagint the Hebrew term *kishsēph* is rendered *pharmakeia,* indicating that the two words mean the same thing.

Since witches, diviners, and sorcerers used drugs, the term *pharmakeia* came to designate witchcraft, enchantment, sorcery, and magic.[13] Even though the law of Moses condemned all such practices and meted out the death penalty for them, this did not prevent their practice. The prophets instructed the people not to consult the mediums and wizards who "chirp" and "mutter." Rather, they should consult God for direct revelation (Isa. 8:19). Both male and female sorcerers who practiced these acts were condemned (Ezek. 13:16–17).

Cases of the practice of sorcery are reported in the New Testament. Simon Magus practiced magic, claiming to be the Messiah. (Messianic tendencies appear to be common among drug users.) But under the preaching of Philip the evangelist, Simon was converted to Christianity and baptized (Acts 8:9, 13). When Sergius Paulus, a proconsul, summoned Barnabas and Saul to hear the word of God, one Elymas, a sorcerer, sought to turn the ruler away from the faith. But Elymas was stricken with blindness, and the proconsul believed in the Lord (Acts 13:6–12).

Paul lists the use of sorcery (*pharmakeia*) as one of the "works of the flesh" and warns that those who practice it will not inherit the Kingdom of God (Gal. 5:20). The apostle saw this practice as a violation of love, which is the basic principle of the Kingdom. Promising freedom, sorcery instead enslaves and deludes its adherents.

Sorcery is also mentioned in Revelation, the last book of the Bible. *Pharmakeia* (employment of drugs in sorcery, magic, enchantment) appears in Rev. 9:21; 18:23. *Pharmakois* ("dealers in drugs") are referred to in ch. 21:8, and *pharmakoi* in ch. 22:15 are also "dealers in drugs." In each case, the sorcerer and sorcery are placed in the categories of murder, theft, deception, idolaters, and those who practice falsehood. Consequently, the sorcerers are placed outside the Kingdom of God.

It should be made clear that the Bible nowhere condemns the use of drugs for healing and health. However, the use of drugs in the practice of magic, sorcery, witchcraft, divination, and the like is emphatically rejected. Such practices were a threat to the Judeo-Christian faith, turning it into superstition and divorcing religion from ethics. Sorcery was, as Stamm notes, "human nature's attempt to compel God to do its bidding instead of praying as Jesus did, 'Thy will be done.'" [14]

3. Biblical Examples of Nondrug-Induced Ecstasy

Nondrug-induced ecstatic experiences are mentioned throughout the Bible. Theophanies occur, visions are seen, and voices are heard by God's people. Theophanic manifestations are largely in the Old Testament. They are accompanied by fire, angels, glory, clouds, and words. For example, God's angel appeared to Moses in the burning bush. Here the theophany includes a vision, an angel, a fire, and a voice (Ex. 3:2–6). In the theophany of Ex., ch. 19, God comes to Israel in a cloud to a people ritually prepared and at the appointed time (Ex. 19:14–16). God also appears to Moses and seventy Israelite nobles (Ex. 24:9–11). Moses is promised a view of God's back, but not his face (Ex. 33:17–23).

The vision is the usual means of God's communication to the prophet. In the remarkable vision of Isaiah, the prophet saw the Lord in his glory and majesty sitting upon a throne. Then he saw himself as a lost and unclean person. After one of the heavenly figures, a seraphim, took a burning coal from the altar and touched the prophet's mouth, his guilt was taken away and he was forgiven. Then he heard the voice of God saying, "Whom shall I send, and who will go for us?" Isaiah responded: "Here am I! Send me." And God said, "Go, and say to this people . . ." (Isa. 6:1–13).

In the New Testament, reference is made to the experience of Moses and the burning bush (Acts 7:30). Accompaniments of theophany are recorded in terms of "fire" (Acts 2:3), "angels" (II Thess. 1:7), "glory" (Luke 2:9); and the Second Coming of Christ is described in theophanic terminology (Matt. 16:27; Mark 8:38; Luke 9:26).

Saul of Tarsus, on the road to Damascus to persecute the Christians, had a direct encounter with God. As Saul approached the city, a light from heaven flashed around him. He fell to the ground and heard a Voice saying to him, "Saul, Saul, why do you persecute me?" Saul asked, "Who are you, Lord?" The Voice answered, "I am Jesus, whom you are persecuting; but rise and enter the city, and you will be told what you are to do." After three days of blindness, Saul could see and immediately began to proclaim Jesus as the Son of God. (Acts 9:1–22.)

The Bible recognizes that mood changes can be accomplished in two basic ways: material and spiritual.[15] Wine can bring about mood elevation, and denial of food can bring depression of mood. On the other hand, obedience to God's will brings mood elevation, whereas disobedience brings depression. The kind of joy and exaltation expressed by the psalmist and other Biblical characters is not produced by any material means. (See Ps. 16:11; Rom. 15:13; I Peter 1:6.) New Testament writers even speak of joy in suffering as well as in salvation (James 1:2; I Peter 4:13). As A. E. Wilder-Smith observes, such mystical joy can fill a person even when in the condition of starvation or mortal agony as the record of martyrs bears out.[16]

Sensory deprivation achieved by fasting is sometimes prerequisite to visions among Biblical characters. Peter had been fasting when he saw the vision of the sheet let down from heaven with different kinds of animals. In this vision he learned that all animals God has cleansed can be eaten and that God shows no partiality toward anyone who fears him (Acts 10:9–35). After his conversion, the apostle Paul went into isolation in Arabia and there had one of many mystical experiences to follow (Acts 16:9; 18:9; 22:17–18; 27:23; Gal. 1:16). On this occasion he was caught up into the "third heaven" (II Cor. 12:1–10). His ecstasy was so great that he lost all sense of physical existence and was unable to tell whether his body was caught up or left on earth. Moreover, he was unable to describe the things he saw. When Paul related such "spiritual trips" to the Corinthians, some of them thought him "beside himself" (II Cor. 5:13).

It is doubtful whether Peter or Paul could hold membership in the average church in America because of their mystical and ecstatic experiences. If they related such experiences, it is possible that they would be looked upon as being "off their rockers." Such ecstatic behavior would not be tolerated. Could it be that today there are some who are turning to psychedelics for ecstasy because it cannot be had in institutionalized religion?

Not only does Christianity offer ecstatic mystico-religious experience without the use of drugs, it also provides mind expansion. To be "in Christ" (this phrase and cognates appear over 150 times in Paul's epistles) is to have the mind of Christ (Phil. 2:2). It is a conscious-ness-expanding experience that views reality from the perspective of Christ and eternity. To have the mind of Christ is to see all men as in him: Jew, Greek, male and female, slave and freeman (Gal. 3:28). To have the mind of Christ is to love all men, to see all history as moving toward a cosmic harmony of men and nature (Eph. 1:10; Col. 1:15–16). To have the mind of Christ is to take his view of sin, judgment, and salvation.

Timothy Leary is right when he declares that "the Christian after rebirth obtains the mind of Christ" (I Cor. 2:16), and that this is a threat to the Establishment.[17] However, he has no Biblical support for his claim that the mystical "in Christ" relationship which results in Christ's gift of his mind comes about by psychedelic drugs. Rather, it is given on the basis of faith, repentance, and commitment to the Lordship of Jesus Christ.

In every instance cited in the Bible, drugs for mind expansion, worship, and the discovery of God are re-jected. The alternative is the discipline of the Holy Spirit. The Christian is to live his "whole life in the Spirit" (Gal. 5:16, Phillips translation). He is to "walk" (conduct), be "led" (counsel), and "live" (companionship) in the Spirit so as not to gratify the desires of the flesh (v. 16, 18, 25). The word "flesh" is more than the body, for it connotes all sinful tendencies, impulses, and de-sires: adultery, fornication, uncleanness, lasciviousness, idolatry, sorcery, enmity, strife, jealousy, anger, selfish-ness, dissension, party spirit, envy, drunkenness, carous-ing, and the like.

In contrast to the "flesh works," the fruit of the Spirit is love, joy, peace, patience, kindness, goodness, faithfulness, gentleness, and self-control—all ethical qualities. These qualities are the result of the indwelling Spirit. Paul urged Christians to get their "high" not from wine (a drug), but from the stimulation of the Spirit (Eph. 5:18).

Dr. Wayne E. Oates has clearly contrasted the experience of the Holy Spirit with that of the psychedelic state. Among other things he notes that the experience of the Holy Spirit arises from a clearly defined community of faith, whereas the psychedelic experience stems from a vague, undefined sense of awe; the former arises from a naturalness, the latter is artificial; the Christian experience is a lifelong pilgrimage, the psychedelic focus is on the "trip," the given moment. The Christian experience defines the nature of one's relationship to God, presenting ethical choices within the scope of one's own development, while drugs do not define the limitations of human existence or the boundaries of human possibility.[18]

By way of recapitulation, the Bible does grant the experience of ecstasy or euphoria, but the use of drugs to facilitate mystical experience is rejected. It recognizes the legitimate use of drugs for health and well-being. The ecstatic experience normally is achieved through the discipline of prayer, meditation, fasting, and the Holy Spirit. And this experience is related to the disclosure of God's will, word, and purpose in history.

CHAPTER 10

THE CHURCH CONFRONTS
THE DRUG CRISIS

THE TRADITIONAL CHURCH stands in the midst of the drug revolution, confused and concerned. It condemns the use of drugs as an aid to the achievement of religious experience. Drugs are rejected by the church as a means toward mind expansion, of awakening agape toward others, or as relief from a sense of alienation and meaninglessness in a drug-oriented society. The church looks askance at the attempt to achieve oneness of the self with God with psychoactive chemicals.

The claim of the drug movement, therefore, to produce mystical experience by a manufactured pill is a threat to the primary mission of the church—to put people in touch with God. If by drugs men can come to know God, then the institutional church may have to fold up in the chemical age.

How is the church to respond to the challenge of the drug culture? Does the church have a theological perspective on drugs? What is its role in the control of the drug traffic and the care of the drug abuser?

1. THE CHURCH AND NARCOTIC RELIGION

Karl Marx, the father of modern communism, summed up the religion of his time by calling it "the opium of the people." [1] By this statement Marx meant that religion was a tool of reaction and an opiate of the people used to calm the desires of the exploited for justice and to ease the consciences of the exploiters. Unfortunately, there is validity in this statement regarding much of the religion of his day and also of that of our contemporary scene.

When the Spanish explorers came to Latin America, they encouraged the Indians there to chew coca leaves, from which cocaine is derived, in order to keep them subdued so that they could be easily dominated and exploited. Likewise, today there is a prevalent kind of church leadership which tends to indoctrinate church members with a cocaine type of religion that makes them insensitive to the problems of drugs, of war, of racism, of poverty, and of political corruption.

The life-style of the church in contemporary society tends to be pietistic and privatized. Its pietistic and otherworldly posture stems from adopting the Greek cosmological view of reality in which the individual strives toward the transcendental in order to escape from an evil world. This is contrary to Hebraic this-worldliness which denies the dichotomy of body and soul. Rather the Judeo-Christian view is that of the unity of the person involved in the world for the cause of love and justice.

This is the heritage of the church, the heritage of a prophetic tradition which looks upon every individual as a person "for whom Christ died" and all men as brothers by creation and redemption. Regardless of a person's condition or class, the church has a mandate to minister to him. But it is not always faithful to this task. Certain groups in society are considered undesirable and unworthy of care. Among these are drug dependents who are too often looked upon as "social lepers" and, therefore, untouchables.

The church must kick its own addiction to class consciousness, to opiate religion which promises "pie in the sky when you die," and to its obsession for self-enhancement. It must mature out of a pro-centric posture in which all action is aimed at constructing bigger buildings, enlarging the budget, increasing the membership for its own self-glory. Rather, the church, to minister effectively today, must take the form of a servant. Its model is that of its Lord who came into the world not to be served but to serve. As Jesus was the "man for others," even so must the church become "pro-existence," that is, for the world and its humanization. This means that the church will work for personal regeneration and social reconstruction.

Instead of anesthetizing church members to the pain of involvement against the forces that dehumanize men, the church must sensitize and activate them to correct these evils and to care for the victims. The model of the New Testament church is not that of an ambulance service which goes only into the field of battle to pick up the wounded. It also has the task of doing battle with the "principalities" and "powers" of which the apostle Paul speaks (Eph. 6:10–20). When the "principalities" and "powers" are demythologized, they are seen to be evil economic, political, and ideological structures. These enemies call for the church to put on the "whole armor of God" for victory.

2. THE CHURCH AND MYSTICISM

Traditionally, the Western Church has been more concerned with the mechanics of institutionalism than with mystical ecstasy, though both Protestants and Catholics have had their great saints. Theresa, Meister Eckhart, John Tauler, and John Ruysbroeck were leading mystics of the Middle Ages. But since the time of Thomas Aquinas (A.D. c. 1225–1274), the Roman Church has tended to react against mysticism and to stress rational knowledge as seen in Scholasticism and in neo-Thomism. Hence, since the days of Aquinas, Catholic mystics have found themselves at odds with their church.

Protestantism has produced few great mystics. Among them are Jakob Böhme, George Fox (founder of Quakerism, which stresses the "inner light" doctrine), and John Woolman. There is a paucity of Protestant mystical literature, except among the Quakers. Protestant mystics, like Catholic mystics, have often been an irritation to the established church; many have found themselves barely tolerated or in some cases excommunicated.

The trend toward the empirical and rational in Western culture has tended to reduce the nonrational in the theology and religious experience of the church. The process of rationalism and secularism has led the churches to attempt to reconcile religion with science and to advance rational proofs of God. The end result is seen in the secularization of faith in the "death of God" theology and in the efforts to develop a secular theology for man "coming of age." Moreover, since religion is popularly viewed as conformity to creeds, little room is left for the mystical.

The trend toward a theology of secularity has resulted in a decline of a sense of the numinous, of religious awe, and of mystical experience. Perhaps Paul Tillich was right when he declared that the question of the century is whether or not man can regain the sense of wonder that he once knew in personal fellowship with the Ground of his Being.[2]

Today the church has largely lost and is sometimes fearful of radical mystical experience. Some of its theologians view with scorn religious ecstasy. The nonrational in religion is rejected with a sense of distrust and even hostility. Hence, the spiritual dimension is missing in many contemporary churches and seminaries.

Modern man, especially the young, is searching for mystical experience. Since man does not find it in the institutional church, he is turning to psychedelic drugs, which he thinks offer him an avenue to an awareness of the holy. In the midst of spiritual sterility, psychedelic cults are turning our young people to chemicals for religious experience.

Because the church shies away from the mystical and rejects drug-induced religious experience, it is being chided by the chemical messiah. He charges the church with doing nothing to provide mystical experience and argues that it can be had in psychedelic drugs. Until the church offers a viable alternative to drug-induced religion, the proponent of the psychedelic cult asserts that the church should not knock the psychedelic scene.

3. TOWARD A THEOLOGICAL PERSPECTIVE
ON THE DRUG PROBLEM

The church's social compassion and concern is rooted in theology. It has done practically no theologizing about drugs because the issue has never been considered a major one. Now the church is left theologically unprepared and without a practical strategy in the midst of a drug crisis. If it is to speak relevantly to the problem and develop effective programs of ministry to drug abusers, the church needs a theology of involvement, a rationale for engagement in the drug culture.

The ultimate basis for Christian concern and action is the God of Biblical revelation. This God discloses himself as the one, true, living God, acting as creator of all things, judge, and redeemer. He reveals himself as a Person, not an impersonal, static Being, who is at work in history, in the lives of men, and in the affairs of nations. His moral demands are in keeping with his own nature: "You shall be holy; for I the Lord your God am holy" (Lev. 19:2; cf. 11:45). God is righteous and requires righteousness of his children (Isa. 45:21; Amos 5:24). Micah, the prophet, sums up in a noble passage the ethical and religious requirements of God:

> He has showed you, O man, what is good;
> and what does the Lord require of you
> but to do justice, and to love kindness,
> and to walk humbly with your God.
>
> (Micah 6:8.)

The God of the Old Testament is supremely disclosed in Jesus Christ, his Son. Jesus is the "visible" image of this "invisible" God (Col. 1:15). In Christ, God became truly human for "the humanization of man." [3] Jesus is pro-man, the "man for others." His compassion and concern embrace all men, the healthy and the sick, the righteous and the unrighteous. His ministry was directed to the poor, the prisoner, the ill, the naked, the hungry, and the oppressed. It is inconceivable that Jesus, who freely mingled with publicans and sinners, would reject a drug abuser.

Man is made in the *imago Dei*, the "image of God," and this fact distinguishes him from all other animals and gives him inherent worth. It follows that any factor, including drugs, which prevents man from becoming fully human is wrong. Forces that dehumanize man, whether they are economic, political, or social are to be confronted by the church with a prophetic gospel and with concrete action. In short, all things that hinder persons in their growth to "mature manhood" measured by the stature of Christ (Eph. 4:13) must be called into question and corrected.

The Holy Spirit is of the same nature as the Father and the Son. "The Lord is the Spirit" (II Cor. 3:17), says Paul, and is the sustainer and moral guide of the Christian. The Spirit is grieved by the sins of the Christian (Eph. 4:30), including the sins against the body, which is "a temple of the Holy Spirit" (I Cor. 6:9–20). For the apostle, the body is not meant to be abused or used for immorality. Rather, the body is "for the Lord, and the Lord for the body" (v. 13). Here, Paul views man as a psychosomatic entity that belongs to God. The term "body" is used as the equivalent of the word "self" or "personality."

Hence, the self constitutes the dwelling place in

which God is to be glorified (I Cor. 6:19–20). Any vice that diminishes personality and sensitivity to spiritual reality is to be strictly avoided. This includes drug abuse, which has deteriorating psychological and physical effects on the abuser and the moral fabric of society.

Another theological teaching that is desperately needed in the contemporary church is that of *koinōnia,* the fellowship of sharing. Though a member of a church, the drug victim may be looked upon by fellow members as a pathetic person who will destroy fellowship. With this sort of attitude on the part of the church, the drug abuser will not be easily convinced that anyone in the congregation understands him or his dilemma. He will not feel that he can bare his guilt to anyone without being rebuffed and rejected. So he turns away from the church.

There is a need for small groups in the church, characterized by a fellowship of sharing and understanding. In these cells the clean as well as the unclean addict can get help to break through the chemical walls that separate him from others. It must be a fellowship in which he can find relationships that make for affection, understanding, and hope. Some examples will be presented later on in this chapter.

Diakonia, or servanthood, must be the shape of the church vis-à-vis the drug culture. Christ who came not to be served but to serve is the model of the church. Jesus came into this world in the form of a servant (Phil. 2:7). Note that he did not come in the disguise of a servant but *became* a servant, in human form, and gave himself on the cross for man's redemption.

This view of Christology has radical implications for the nature and functions of the church. Just as Christ took the form of a servant, even so must the church. This involves self-emptying, service, and solidarity with humanity. This means that the church to *be* the church must take the form of Christ in the world. There is a basic difference in going *to* church and *being* the church. To be the church is not only to worship in a building, but to minister to one's fellowman where he works, plays, lives, and dies. The church, or "the people of God," are to become engaged in the world where God is at work redeeming and reconciling men to himself and to one another. Wherever men stand in need of help and healing, there is where the church is to be.

4. New Forms of Ministry

The Christological view of Jesus as servant is to be the shape of the church in a secular society. Jesus ministered to human need wherever he found it. In order to follow his example, the church must get out of the narrow confines of its meetinghouse and into the world of human need and suffering. The church must give up its frenetic concern for little churchinesses and expand its ministry to that socially taboo area called the drug scene.

It is encouraging to note that some traditional or institutional churches are beginning to develop new forms of ministry to drug abusers. For example, a church in Florida provides sessions for parents and teen-agers in which there are open discussions about drug abuse. In addition, there is a weekly meeting of the young people who have been drug users and are trying to stay clean. This group meets weekly and the program is patterned somewhat after Alcoholics Anonymous. Of this group, two nineteen-year-old girls who were on drugs speak in the various civic clubs of the city. The Kiwanis Club provides three committees: one to get jobs for the youth who are staying off drugs, one for drug education, and another for a halfway house. Rather than go to jail, the young people who have been arrested for drug abuse can be sentenced to the halfway house for a program of rehabilitation.

Through the local newspapers and TV, information about drugs is provided to help the public recognize the symptoms of young people who are using drugs. The pastor and his assistants work in cooperation with the guidance center in the city where several doctors offer their services to help drug abusers. This ministry has received quite a bit of publicity, and the young people know that if they want to get off drugs, they can participate in the program.

A church in the Park Slope area of Brooklyn, New York, is experimenting with several forms of ministry to youth. A coffeehouse is maintained from 8:00 P.M. to 11:00 P.M. each day. This coffeehouse is a means of getting people involved in dialogue, workshops, and creative arts as an extension of the program. The Psyche Morning has been established. After the coffeehouse closes at 11:00 P.M., the community room is opened for individual and/or small-group dialogue and/or counseling. Here young people let themselves go by stating what is on their mind, revealing their hang-ups, and discussing their dilemma concerning religion and religious beliefs.

Another interesting feature of the program of the Brooklyn church is called the Catacombs. It is a sort of Christian discotheque featuring local bands and dancing on Saturday night. The young people of the community were instrumental in getting the Catacombs started by building, painting, wiring, and designing the facility.

The Catacombs is patterned after the Electric Circus in the East Village of New York, but with Christian overtones in its operation. Located in the basement of the church, the Catacombs accommodates over two hundred people. Psychedelic lighting is used to bring out color and to provide atmosphere. Projectors are used to show slides with Christian motifs on the wall.

Many of these young people who gather in the Catacombs are on drugs. About 70 percent of the young people in the Park Slope area of Brooklyn are experimenting with drugs, and about 30 percent of them are addicts. The Drug Addiction Services, an agency established by Mayor Lindsay to combat the problem of drugs in the metropolitan area of New York City, provides training for those who are interested in helping combat the drug problem. This agency also provides educational programs for teen-agers, teaching them the effects of drugs on the mind and body. Also, the DAS helps to establish rehabilitation centers in communities where there is an interest in such a program. The Park Slope church is working with this agency in order to obtain facilities and staff members for a rehabilitation center for drug addicts in the Park Slope area. The church is making use of the facilities of this agency for personnel training and as a resource for obtaining drug information for the community.

The East Harlem Protestant Parish in 1956 established the East Harlem Parish Narcotics Committee to provide personal and professional service to drug addicts. The Committee is made up of representatives of seven Protestant denominations and other Protestant groups. The

Narcotics Committee offers addicts recreation and psychiatric, medical, and social services as well as spiritual help. When entering hospitals, addicts are provided guidance for admittance and are later visited and counseled. Help is also available in finding food, lodging, and jobs for drug abusers. A sign on the door of the East Harlem Protestant Parish depicts a cross smashing a hypodermic syringe, indicating the goal of the program. Through professional and spiritual assistance, thousands of addicts have been helped in their efforts to kick the drug habit.

Some churches are employing ministers to work specifically with the drug abusers. For example, a church in Louisville, Kentucky, has employed a minister full time to work specifically in the drug culture. He understands the drug problem and is officially connected with the Drug Abuse Information and Education Center of the city. There are three basic factors in his program. First, there is visibility. He is present in person. He stations himself in the parks, drive-ins, and eating places of the streets where young people gather. His clerical collar identifies him, but does not create a barrier between him and the youths. Secondly, there is availability. He is on the job twenty-four hours a day. His phone may ring at any hour of the night, and the young people know that he will listen when they call. In the third place, there is the factor of credibility. He is always himself and expresses genuine concern for the spiritual welfare of drug users.

When the young people ask this minister why he is so concerned about them, he replies that he loves people. He then tells them about Jesus. However, he does not take an "evangelistic approach," which he thinks would be phony and that young people would quickly detect it. In short, he doesn't attempt to "push Jesus" on the young people. One thing he insists upon when he is with drug users is that they refrain from having drugs in their possession. No drugs can be brought into his home or transported on anyone's person in his automobile. The minister could be coindicted if he were with a person possessing drugs at the time of arrest by the police.

The goal of this pastor is to enable the teen-agers to face up to their behavior and change it. As he sees it, his job is that of trying to help them overcome the feelings of inadequacy, hopelessness, and insecurity which have led to their use of drugs. So far, he has succeeded in helping a number of young people to kick the habit and also in getting runaways to go back home and start life over again.[4]

Some persons perform a unique ministry to drug abusers on their own. Earth-Mother is the name by which a middle-aged woman is affectionately known among the drug culture of Louisville, Kentucky. ("Earth-Mother" was the bountiful goddess of the ancient Peruvians from whom came forth earth's fruits.) For more than twenty years she has been working with young people, trying to get them off drugs. In the beginning, she worked out of her apartment in the community, with the focus of her ministry in Cherokee Park, where young people gather each evening.

Earth-Mother now has a large three-story brick structure in a salubrious section of the city. It is called All the Way House and has ten young drug abusers as residents. Their ages range from sixteen to twenty, with a predominance of males. Residents stay at the house three weeks for "treatment." The schedule is a rugged one. Everyone gets up at 6:00 in the morning. After devotions, they all eat breakfast at 7:00, then work until 10:30. Each has a job, such as cooking, washing dishes, cleaning house, painting, and repairing. At 10:30 all gather for Bible study. After lunch there is free time until 3:00, when another Bible study period begins. From 4:00 to 6:00 there is another work period. Dinner is served at 6:30, followed by a "gripe session" and an attic chapel service at 8:00 o'clock. Lights are out at 11:00.

All youths hooked on drugs get the cold turkey treatment, and no drugs are allowed on the premises. Earth-Mother refuses to allow the house to become a crashpad for drug abusers. The police of the city know her and think that her approach is one of many necessary to deal with the drug problem.

During the three weeks of treatment, no one can leave the house except with the whole group, which attends church together. After three weeks in the house, the individual may secure a job. If he so chooses, he may spend his nights in the house or somewhere else.

All the Way House is near Cherokee Park and Hogan's Fountain where Earth-Mother sustains her ministry to the young drug abusers who gather there. Her phone number is passed around among the youths, and she is on emergency call twenty-four hours each day. She sees her task as twofold: to help youngsters get off the wrong road, the way of drugs, and to get them on the right road, the way of the love of Jesus. She claims that her program is a "Christ-centered" one and insists that it takes tremendous power to kick the drug habit. For her, this power is "the baptism of the Holy Spirit." By this she means total commitment to Christ. She says that many of those who go through the program at All the Way House do become "clean" and follow Jesus.[5]

A new group known as "Jesus Freaks," made up of youth disillusioned with drugs, has appeared on the West Coast. They have established more than a hundred communes for Bible believers from the State of Washington to Southern California. These communes are known as Jesus houses or Christian houses and bear such names as the Fish House, Port of Call, Tree of Life, and the House of Pergamos.

Based on a fundamentalist theology, the movement feels that organized religion, including most fundamentalist churches, has become sterile and unspiritual. It is a sort of postdrug fundamentalist revival which, during the last two years, has turned on hundreds of young people. Declared one college dropout who works full time in the movement: "Lots of youth are freaked-out on drugs and meditation or Zen. We've been through that and weren't satisfied. Now we are freaked-out on Jesus." [6]

Most of the Jesus Freaks have dropped out of the middle-class culture and found a satisfying style of life in "following Jesus." They have all the marks of the hippie culture, but have rejected its ideals as well as those of the straight culture. It is their aim to follow the injunction of Jesus to be "in the world, but not of the world." A communal life-style has been adopted because they think that was the pattern of early Christians. Unlike the hippies, these young people live in neatly kept houses in residential areas. Some are strictly communal, with married couples pooling their worldly goods. Others serve as crashpads, where young people spend the night and hear the gospel preached by permanent residents.

These are the young people who have become disillusioned with the drug experience. Their spiritual hunger has led them to a fundamentalist type of Christianity. "I realize that the visions I had under drugs were visions of myself, not God," asserted one ex-drug abuser. "Then I found Jesus," he said, "and it's a whole different kind of trip. . . . It really blew my mind." [7]

"Turn on with Jesus—it's a good trip," "Jesus saves," "the Eternal Rush," are among the slogans inscribed on the jackets and automobiles of the Jesus Freaks.

5. FACT-FINDING AND SOCIAL ACTION

Generally speaking, the church is not equipped with the facts to deal realistically with this age of psychochemistry. As in the case of so many critical issues, it has been more of a "taillight" than a "headlight." Its rearview-mirror approach to reality has left the church disarmed in its ministry to the drug culture.

One of the first tasks of the churches is to educate themselves about the facts and fictions of drug abuse. This will involve more than routine discussions and visits to halfway houses. A thorough study of the solid literature in the field of drug abuse coupled with creative ways of rehabilitating those who are hooked on drugs is required. It is a tragic fact that there are so few resources dealing with the drug issue from the Christian perspective. Religious film resources too often oversimplify and overdramatize the problem. Too much of the religious literature in the field is heavily moralistic and lacks facticity. What is needed is some theological research "carefully coordinated with relevant scientific research." [8] In other words, the approach to the drug problem must be a bifocal one. This means that the theologian must look to the scientist, the sociologist, and the psychologist for factual data as to *what is* and to the norms of revelation for insight into *what ought to be* in relation to the drug problem.

Cooperation of the churches with other agencies in the community coping with the drug problem is essential. No one agency or institution can handle the problem alone. A coordinated effort of all the community agencies and resources is needed.

In California, for example, a hot line is in operation. The citizens of Palos Verdes have hired a full-time narcotics education official (salary $16,000) and set up a twenty-four-hour-a-day hot line, which troubled parents or children can use to call one of four churches for assistance. Depending upon the seriousness of the case, the caller is referred to a group-therapy session, a minister, or a psychiatrist. More than a dozen doctors, lawyers, and ministers are contributing their time.[9]

The pastor is the key person to initiate ministries to drug victims. He himself must become knowledgeable about the problems. He must also know something of the techniques of counseling. One of the first principles in counseling the addicted person is to listen to him and not lecture to him. It is fatal for the pastor to attempt to impress the addict with his own knowledge of drugs. Rather, the minister's main task is to help the addicted person to find alternative nondrug ways of handling hang-ups, anxiety, guilt, and boredom.

Every pastor should view the drug addict as a spiritually sick person and treat him as such. Rev. Norman Eddy, chairman of the New York Council of Narcotic Addiction, has pointed out that no matter what professionals may say about the problem, addiction to drugs "is a symptom of a deep-rooted spiritual sickness, and a diabolical answer to the spiritual quest of the man without faith in God." [10]

The pastor must play a supporting role in relation to the family of the drug abuser. Parents become frustrated and sometimes angry when their children turn to drugs. Their suffering is intense and agonizing. The pastor can help these parents and members of the family to understand the drug dependent and to relate themselves constructively to him.

The minister must work with community resources designed to aid the drug addict. He should become acquainted with the drug-abuse information centers, the clinics, doctors, lawyers, law enforcement officers, and others from which he can get help.

Above all, the minister must have the conviction that many people can be released from the bondage of addiction only by the power of God. He must see each person as a person "for whom Christ died." With this conviction in mind, he will lead his church to participate in the mission of Christ: "To proclaim release to the captives and recovering of sight to the blind, to set at liberty those who are oppressed" (Luke 4:18).

DRUG JARGON

THE DRUG CULTURE has a language all its own. The following glossary attempts to present those terms which will be helpful to the layman who is unfamiliar with the special jargon by which drug abusers communicate. Of course, the nondrug user also employs some of these terms and they cannot be considered as evidence that he is a drug abuser.

ACID—LSD (lysergic acid diethylamide), a powerful psychedelic drug.

ACIDHEAD—an LSD abuser; also, cubehead.

ACID ROCK—rock and roll music inspired by and compatible with the LSD experience.

BABYSIT—to guide one through his drug experience.

BAD TRIP—a bad experience with a psychedelic drug; also called a bum trip or a bummer.

BAG—a package of drugs; a particular drug or thing that appeals to one.

BANG—to inject or "shoot" drugs.

BARBS—barbiturates.

BENNIES—Benzedrine.

BLOW YOUR MIND—to alter radically one's consciousness; to become high on drugs.

BREAD—money.

BUSTED—arrested by the police.

BURNED—to be cheated in a drug purchase.

BUTTONS—peyote buttons or the surface growth of the peyote plant.

CAP—capsule.

CHIPPING—ingesting drugs occasionally.

COLD TURKEY—abrupt withdrawal from narcotics (from resulting gooseflesh which resembles the skin of a plucked turkey).

CONNECTION—a supplier of drugs.

COOKER—a spoon used to prepare or to cook heroin before injection.

COMING DOWN—recovering from a trip or a high on drugs.

COP OUT—to quit, to alibi, to defect.

CRASHPAD—a place for the drug abuser to live and sleep.

CRYSTAL—Methedrine or methamphetamine.

CUT—to dilute drugs, especially narcotics.

CUT OUT—to depart, to leave, to split.

DEALER—drug peddler.

DIG—to enjoy, to understand, to approve.

DIME BAG—ten dollars' worth of narcotics.

DMT—dimethyltryptamine, a drug similar to LSD.

DOPE—generally any drug, but especially narcotics.

DOPER—an addict.

DOWNERS—barbiturates, sedatives.

DROP—to swallow a drug.

DYNAMITE—a powerful drug of any kind.

FED—a federal narcotics officer.

FINK—to inform on someone to the police or the Establishment.

FIX—an injection of narcotics.

FREAKOUT—to lose touch with reality while on drugs.

FUZZ—the police.

GLUE SNIFFING—inhaling organic solvents such as model-airplane glue.

GOOD TRIP—a happy experience with a psychedelic drug.

GOOF BALLS—barbiturates.

GRASS—marijuana.

GUIDE—anyone not on drugs who sits with another person under the influence of LSD.

H—heroin.

HABIT—addiction to drugs.

HANG-UP—any personal problem that troubles one.

HASHISH—the most concentrated form of marijuana.

HEARTS—amphetamines that are heart-shaped.

HIGH—intoxicated on drugs.

HOOKED—addicted to drugs.

JOINT—a marijuana cigarette.

JUNK—heroin.

JUNKIE—a narcotics user.

KICK THE HABIT—to stop using drugs.

KICKS—the pleasant effects of drugs.

KIT—equipment for injecting drugs; also, layout, machinery, artillery.

KNOCKOUT DROPS—chloral hydrate, a sedative.

LID—one ounce of marijuana.

LIPTON TEA—a poor quality of heroin.

LOCO WEED—marijuana.

MAINLINE—to inject drugs directly into the veins.

MAN—the police.

MESCAL BEANS—mescaline or peyote.

MESCALINE—drug from peyote.

MONKEY ON THE BACK—drug addiction; a monkey on the back which must be fed.

NARC, NARCO—a narcotics officer.

OD—overdose of narcotics.

ON THE NOD—under the influence of drugs.

PANIC—scarcity of drugs.

PEP PILLS—amphetamines.

POP—to inject drugs subcutaneously; skin popping.

POT—marijuana.

POTHEAD—chronic user of marijuana.

PURPLE HEARTS—Dexamyl.

PUSHER—drug peddler.

RAP—to discuss, to communicate.

RED BIRDS, RED DEVILS—Seconal (barbiturate).

REEFER—a marijuana cigarette.

ROACH—the butt of a marijuana cigarette.

ROACH HOLDER—device for holding a marijuana cigarette so that it can be smoked to the end without burning one's fingers.

ROPE—marijuana.

SCENE—the place where the action is; the drug scene.

SCORE—to make a drug purchase.

SHOOT UP—to inject drugs.

SKIN POPPING—to inject drugs under the skin instead of in a vein.

SNORT—to sniff or inhale drugs, usually heroin or cocaine, through the nose.

SPEED—Methedrine, which is usually injected and produces a powerful high.

SPEEDBALL—an injection of a powerful drug, usually a combination of heroin and cocaine.

SPEEDFREAK—one who habitually uses speed.

SPIKE—a hypodermic needle.

STASH—a hidden supply of drugs.

STONED—under the influence of drugs or alcohol.

STP—Serenity, Tranquility, Peace—a drug mixture of

Methedrine and psychedelic compounds.

STRAIGHT—a nonuser of drugs who belongs to the Establishment.

STRUNG OUT—heavily addicted to drugs.

TOKE UP—to light a marijuana cigarette.

TRACKS—scars along the veins caused by needle injections.

TRIP—to become intoxicated on drugs, usually psychedelics.

TURN ON—to use drugs; to introduce someone else to drugs.

UNDERGROUND—the drug subculture.

UPTIGHT—to be nervous, tense, anxious.

UPPERS—amphetamines.

WIG—the mind.

WIG OUT—to blow one's mind.

WINGDING—pretended withdrawal symptoms in order to get a doctor to give one narcotics.

WINGS—the first mainline injection of a narcotic.

WITHDRAWAL SYNDROME—symptoms of aches, tears, running nose, gooseflesh, nausea, diarrhea, muscle cramps, etc., accompanying abrupt withdrawal of a drug from someone physically dependent upon it.

YELLOW JACKETS—Nembutal (barbiturate).

FILM RESOURCES

Bennies and Goofballs, 16mm. film, sound, black and white, 20 minutes. As the title indicates, this film deals with the abuse of amphetamine and barbiturate drugs. Voices of drug abusers whose lives have been marred by these drugs lend realism and authenticity to the presentation. It is beamed to young people from senior high school through college. Available from Bureau of Narcotics and Dangerous Drugs, 1405 I Street, N.W., Washington, D.C. 20537.

Hide and Seek, 16mm. film, sound, color, 14 minutes. This film depicts a real-life teen-ager hooked on narcotics and unable to shake the habit. It is suitable for persons from junior high through college. Available from Center for Mass Communication, Columbia University Press, 440 W. 11th Street, New York, N.Y. 10025.

Hooked, 16mm. film, sound, black and white, 20 minutes. In this film, young people relate why they came to use drugs, how usage affected their relationships with others, and why they feel disgust from the drug experience. It is suitable for persons between the ages of eighteen and twenty-five. Produced by and available from Churchill Films, 662 N. Robertson Boulevard, Los Angeles, Calif. 90069.

Escape to Nowhere, 16mm. film, sound, color, 27 minutes. The real-life story of a teen-age girl named Debbie is presented in this film. It tells of her futile effort to find a solution to her problems by using drugs. An open-ended story, it is designed to provoke dialogue and to stimulate questions. Released in 1968, it is beamed to senior high school and college students. Available from Professional Arts, Inc., P.O. Box 8484, Universal City, Calif. 91608.

LSD: Insight or Insanity? 16mm. film, sound, color, 18 minutes. Perhaps a bit overdramatized, this film focuses upon the abuse of LSD. Sidney Cohen explains why young people take LSD, and the possible damage to the human chromosomes is indicated and also the possible effects upon an unborn child when LSD is taken during pregnancy. Suitable for showing to junior high school, high school, and college students. Available from BFA Education Media, 2211 Michigan Avenue, Santa Monica, Calif. 90404.

LSD-25, 16mm. film, sound, color, 27 minutes. This is an objective and informative film about LSD, including the reaction of persons under its influence. Honored by the American Film Library Association, *LSD-25* is void of scare tactics and moralistic preachments. Since the film describes the potency of LSD and the unpredictable results that may occur when it is ingested, viewers should be convinced that it is indeed a dangerous drug. Released by Professional Arts, Inc.

The Riddle, 16mm. film, sound, black and white, 20 minutes. Drug abusers, including glue sniffers and heroin addicts, are filmed in the authentic drug scene. Rock and roll music provides the appropriate atmosphere, and the frank comments of the drug abusers add to the force of the film. The aim of the film is to deglamorize drug abuse. Suitable for junior high through college students. National Audiovisual Center, Washington, D.C. 20409.

Marijuana, 16mm. film, sound, color, 34 minutes. A teen-age pot party is raided by the police. The smokers present the most common arguments for using marijuana. These arguments are answered by teen-agers themselves, with the help of a person named Sonny Bono. Interviews also occur in which young people present their candid reasons for rejecting the culture of adults. There are also interviews with teen-agers who do not use drugs. The film is open-ended, leaving the decision about the use of marijuana to the individual viewer. Available from BFA Education Media.

BUREAU OF NARCOTICS
AND DANGEROUS DRUGS

INFORMATION on drugs and drug abuse is provided upon request from the Bureau of Narcotics and Dangerous Drugs in Washington (1405 "I" Street, N.W. Washington, D.C. 20537) and at the following district offices:

Region I, JFK Federal Bldg., Room E-311, Boston, Mass. 02203

Region II, 90 Church Street, Suite 605, New York, N.Y. 10007

Region III, 605 U.S. Custom House, 2d and Chestnut Streets, Philadelphia, Pa. 19106

Region IV, 31 Hopkins Place, Room 945, Baltimore, Md. 21201

Region V, 1515 N.W. 7th Street, Room 205, Miami, Fla. 33125

Region VI, 602 Federal Bldg. and U.S. Courthouse, 231 W. Lafayette, Detroit, Mich. 48226

Region VII, Engineering Bldg., Suite 1700, 206 W. Wacker Drive, Chicago, Ill. 60606

Region VIII, 939 Federal Office Bldg., 600 South Street, New Orleans, La. 70130

Region IX, Federal Office Bldg., 110 South Fourth Street, Minneapolis, Minn. 55401

Region X, Suite 115, U.S. Courthouse, 811 Grand, Kansas City, Mo. 64106

Region XI, Room 723, 1114 Commerce, Dallas, Tex. 75202

Region XII, New Custom House, 1950 Stout Street, Denver, Colo. 80202

Region XIII, 311 U.S. Courthouse, Seattle, Wash. 98104

Region XIV, Petroleum Bldg., 714 W. Olympic Blvd., Suite 1010, Los Angeles, Calif. 90015

NOTES

PREFACE

1. Richard Alpert, Sidney Cohen, and Lawrence Schiller, *LSD,* p. 19.

2. *Ibid.,* p. 20.

Chapter 1. A DRUG-ORIENTED SOCIETY

1. Roland Berg, "Why Americans Hide Behind a Chemical Curtain," *Look,* Aug. 8, 1967, p. 12.

2. Joel Fort, "The Drug Revolution," *Playboy,* Feb., 1970, p. 66.

3. *Newsweek,* Feb. 9, 1970, pp. 28–29.

4. "Pop Drugs: The High as a Way of Life," *Time,* Sept. 26, 1969, p. 68.

5. Berg, *loc. cit.,* p. 17.

6. James T. Carey, *The College Drug Scene,* p. 66.

7. Tom Lyons, "The Peculiar Conformist," *Thoroughbred Magazine,* Vol. 1, 1970 (University of Louisville), pp. 3–7.

8. "The Drug Scene: High Schools Are Higher Now," *Newsweek,* Feb. 16, 1970, p. 66.

9. *Ibid.*

10. *The Louisville Times,* June 12, 1970, p. 1.

11. "Kids and Heroin: The Adolescent Epidemic," *Time,* March 16, 1970, p. 16.

12. "Drug Menace: How Serious?" *U.S. News & World Report,* May 25, 1970, p. 38.

13. *The Courier-Journal and Times,* June 21, 1970, p. A-1.

14. "Marijuana—the Other Enemy in Vietnam," *U.S. News & World Report,* Jan. 26, 1970, pp. 68–69.

15. *The Courier-Journal and Times,* Feb. 22, 1970, p. A-6.

16. "Does Our Army Fight on Drugs?" *Look,* June 16, 1970, p. 75.

17. "The Pot Bust," *Newsweek,* May 11, 1970, p. 95.

18. John Filiatreau, "Fountain of Youth," *The Courier-Journal,* June 6, 1970, p. 1.

19. Donald B. Louria, *Nightmare Drugs* (Pocket Books, Inc., 1966), pp. 76–77.

Chapter 2. DRUG IDENTIFICATION

1. *Webster's New World Dictionary of the American Language,* College Edition (The World Publishing Company, 1964), p. 445.

2. W. Modell, "Mass Drug Catastrophies and the Roles of Science and Technology," *Science,* April 21, 1967, p. 346.

3. Richard R. Lingeman, *Drugs from A to Z: A Dictionary,* p. 58.

4. Sidney Cohen, *The Drug Dilemma,* p. 8.

5. Lingeman, *op. cit.,* pp. 58–59.

6. S. Cohen, *The Drug Dilemma,* p. 10.

7. Alton Blakeslee, *What You Should Know About Drugs and Narcotics* (Association Press, 1969), p. 16.

8. For a detailed study of the effect of LSD on normal subjects, see Abram Hoffer and Humphrey Osmond, *The Hallucinogens* (Academic Press, Inc., 1967), pp. 110–127.

9. John Cashman, *The LSD Story* (Fawcett Publications, Inc., 1966), pp. 84–85.

10. Maimon M. Cohen, *et al.,* "Chromosomal Damage in Human Leukocytes Induced by Lysergic Acid Diethylamide," *Science,* March 17, 1967, pp. 1417–1419.

11. G. J. Alexander, *et al.,* "LSD: Injection Early in Pregnancy Produces Abnormalities in Offspring of Rats," *Science,* July 28, 1967, pp. 459–460.

12. See Edward R. Bloomquist, *Marijuana,* for an excellent treatment of this drug.

13. Robert P. Walton, *Marijuana: America's New Drug Problem* (J. B. Lippincott Company, 1938), pp. 125–126.

14. Bloomquist, *op. cit.*, p. 199.

15. See James S. Slotkin, *The Peyote Religion.*

16. See Hoffer and Osmond, *op. cit.*, pp. 480–500.

17. See Robert Graves, "The Divine Rite of Mushrooms," *Atlantic*, Feb., 1970, p. 109.

18. John P. Fort, Jr., "Heroin Addiction Among Young Men," in John A. O'Donnell and John C. Ball (eds.), *Narcotic Addiction*, pp. 84–85.

Chapter 3. DYNAMICS OF DRUG ABUSE

1. John G. Saxe, "The Blind Men and the Elephant," in *The Poems of John Godfrey Saxe* (Houghton Mifflin and Company, 1882), p. 136.

2. *The Courier-Journal and Times,* March 16, 1969, Section B-1.

3. *The Courier-Journal and Times,* April 12, 1970, Section G-1.

4. David P. Ausubel, *Drug Addiction: Physiological, Psychological, and Sociological Aspects,* p. 42.

5. Carey, *op. cit.*, pp. 122–132.

6. *The Courier-Journal and Times,* Feb. 22, 1970, p. A-6.

7. S. Cohen, *The Drug Dilemma,* p. 119.

8. Cf. John C. Cooper, *The New Mentality* (The Westminster Press, 1969), p. 62.

9. James R. Allen, "Flight from Violence: Hippies and the Green Rebellion," *American Journal of Psychiatry,* Sept. 1968, p. 365.

10. "Kids and Heroin," *Time,* March 16, 1970, p. 17.

11. *Ibid.*, p. 19.

12. "Life on Two Grams a Day," *Life,* March 20, 1970, p. 39.

13. *The Denver Post,* Feb. 3, 1970, p. 3.

14. See Frank Barron, "Motivational Patterns in LSD," in Richard C. DeBold and Russell C. Leaf (eds.), *LSD, Man and Society,* pp. 3–4.

15. Bloomquist, *op. cit.*, p. 135.

16. *Ibid.*

17. "The Periscope," *Newsweek,* May 1, 1970.

18. Timothy Leary, *High Priest,* "Acknowledgements."

19. "A Father Tells How Drugs Invaded His Family," *Life,* March 20, 1970, p. 56.

Chapter 4. LEGAL CONTROL OF DRUGS

1. For details, see Henry J. Anslinger and W. F. Tompkins, *The Traffic in Narcotics* (Funk & Wagnalls Company, 1953), Appendix I, pp. 318–331.

2. Paul A. Pumpian, *The Food and Drug Administration and the Drug Abuse Control Amendments,* NASPA Background Paper, pp. 1–4.

3. *Ibid.*

4. Helen H. Nowlis, *Drugs on the College Campus,* p. 46.

5. *The Denver Post,* Feb. 2, 1970, p. 18.

6. Bloomquist, *op. cit.,* pp. 134–135.

7. "Kids and Heroin," *Time,* March 16, 1970, pp. 20 ff.

8. Rudolph Chelminski, "Open Season on Drug Smugglers," *Life,* June 26, 1970, p. 33.

9. Alfred R. Lindesmith, *The Addict and the Law,* p. 234.

10. *Life,* Oct. 31, 1969, p. 34.

11. *Newsweek,* July 24, 1967, p. 47.

12. "Drug Menace: How Serious?" *U.S. News & World Report,* May 25, 1970, p. 41.

13. "Toward a Perspective on Marijuana," *Wall Street Journal,* March 25, 1968, p. 2.

14. Bloomquist, *op. cit.,* p. 199.

15. See Walton, *op. cit.,* p. 121; Gerard Piel, "Narcotics," *Life,* July 19, 1943; C. Knight Aldrich, "The Effects of a Synthetic Marijuana-like Compound on Musical Talent," *Public Health Report,* Vol. 59 (March 31, 1944), pp. 431–433.

16. Bloomquist, *op. cit.,* p. 169.

17. Lingeman, *op. cit.,* p. 150.

18. See Robert S. De Ropp, *Drugs and the Mind,* pp. 102 f.

19. Mayor LaGuardia's Committee on Marijuana, "The Marijuana Problem in the City of New York," in David Solomon (ed.), *The Marijuana Papers,* p. 41.

20. Ausubel, *op. cit.*, p. 98.

21. Bloomquist, *op. cit.*, p. 185.

22. *Ibid.*, p. 169.

23. Address to the Governors' Conference in Washington, D.C., Dec., 1969.

24. *Life*, Oct. 31, 1969, pp. 30–31.

25. M. P. Rosenthal, "Proposals for Dangerous Drug Legislation," *Task Force Report: Narcotics and Drug Abuse,* President's Commission on Law Enforcement and the Administration of Justice (U.S. Government Printing Office, 1967).

26. See "But I Wasn't Smoking It," *Home Life Magazine,* June, 1970, pp. 12–16.

27. *Life,* Oct. 31, 1969, p. 34.

28. Louria, *Nightmare Drugs*, p. 36.

29. Cited by Bloomquist, *op. cit.*, p. 149.

Chapter 5. PARENTS AND THE DRUG PROBLEM

1. Remarks by Art Linkletter at the White House before a bipartisan leadership discussion on the narcotic problem.

2. Isidore Chein, *et al., The Family Addict* (Research Center for Human Relations, 1956), p. 37.

3. P. Zimmering, "Drug Addiction in Relation to the Problem of Adolescence," *American Journal of Psychiatry,* Oct., 1952, pp. 272–278.

4. "How Can You Tell if Your Child Is Taking Drugs?" *Look,* April 7, 1970, p. 44.

Chapter 6. RESOURCES FOR REHABILITATION

1. G. A. Hunt and N. E. Odoroff, "Follow-up Study of Narcotic Drug Addicts After Hospitalization," *Public Health Report,* No. 77, 1962.

2. Barbara Leslie Austin, *Sad Nun at Synanon* (Holt, Rinehart and Winston, Inc., 1970).

3. From the printed program *The Concept,* presented by the Smithsonian Associates and the Division of Performing Arts, Jan. 18 and 19, 1970, Smithsonian Institution, Washington, D.C.

4. See the booklet *Some One Close to You Is on Drugs,* published by the City of New York Human Resources Administration Addiction Services Agency, 71 Worth Street, New York, N.Y., 10013, for the full story of all the programs.

5. *Ibid.*

6. *Ibid.*

7. *American Journal of Psychiatry,* April, 1970, p. 1553.

8. *Ibid.,* pp. 1552–1553.

Chapter 7. DRUGS AND RELIGIOUS EXPERIENCE

1. William R. Inge, *Christian Mysticism* (London: Methuen and Co., Ltd., 1948), pp. 335–348.

2. William James, *The Varieties of Religious Experience,* p. 292.

3. Walter T. Stace, *Mysticism and Philosophy,* pp. 110 f.

4. See Timothy Leary, *High Priest.*

5. —— "The Religious Experience: Its Production and Interpretation," *Dialog,* Summer, 1964, p. 215.

6. Sidney Cohen, *The Beyond Within: The LSD Story,* p. 225.

7. Cashman, *op. cit.,* p. 62.

8. Leary, *loc. cit.,* p. 216.

9. *Ibid.*

10. *Ibid.,* p. 218.

11. *Ibid.,* pp. 218–219.

12. *Ibid.,* p. 220.

13. Walter N. Pahnke, "LSD and Religious Experience," in DeBold and Leaf (eds.), *op. cit.,* pp. 63–64.

14. For a detailed account of the experiment, see Walter N. Pahnke, "Drugs and Mysticism: An Analysis of the Relationship Between Psychedelic Drugs and the Mystical Consciousness."

15. Pahnke, "LSD and Religious Experience," in DeBold and Leaf (eds.), *op. cit.,* p. 82.

16. Walter H. Clark, *Chemical Ecstasy: Psychedelic Drugs and Religion.*

17. *Ibid.,* vi.

18. *Ibid.,* p. 132.

19. *Ibid.,* pp. 149–151.

20. *Ibid.,* p. 165.

21. See Huston Smith, *The Religions of Man* (Harper & Brothers, 1958), p. 51.

22. Clark, *op. cit.,* p. 44; for the full story on peyote religion, see Slotkin, *op. cit.,* and David F. Aberle, *The Peyote Religion Among the Navaho* (Aldine Publishing Company, 1966).

23. Cited from the court ruling by Neil L. Chayet, "Social and Legal Aspects of LSD Usage," in DeBold and Leaf (eds.), *op. cit.,* p. 105.

24. William Braden, *The Private Sea: LSD and the Search for God,* pp. 90, 174.

25. *Ibid.,* pp. 174–175.

26. Cited by Huston Smith, "Psychedelic Theophanies and the Religious Life," *Christianity and Crisis,* June 26, 1967, p. 144.

27. *Ibid.,* pp. 174–175.

28. Leary, *High Priest,* under "Note" in flyleaf.

29. *Ibid.*

30. *Ibid.,* p. 2.

31. *Ibid.,* p. 3.

32. *Ibid.*

33. Timothy Leary, *Psychedelic Prayers* (Poets Press, 1966).

34. Braden, *op. cit.,* pp. 47–48.

Chapter 8. PSYCHEDELIC RELIGION: FACT OR FANTASY

1. David Ebin (ed.), *The Drug Experience,* pp. 16, 39.

2. Clark, *op. cit.,* p. 89.

3. Ebin, *op. cit.,* p. 37.

4. Smith, *loc cit.,* p. 145.

5. "God and Drugs," in Hal Bridges, *American Mysticism from William James to Zen,* p. 151.

6. R. E. L. Masters and Jean Houston, *The Varieties of Psychedelic Experience,* p. 123.

7. *Ibid.,* p. 126.

8. See A. H. Becker, "What the Minister Ought to Know About LSD," *Pastoral Psychology,* Oct., 1965, p. 45.

9. Masters and Houston, *op. cit.,* p. 126.

10. *Ibid.,* p. 127.

11. Ebin, *op. cit.,* pp. 37–40.

12. Smith, *loc. cit.,* p. 145.

13. *Ibid.,* p. 146.

14. *Ibid.,* p. 147.

15. Lawrence Schiller, *The Killing of Sharon Tate* (The New American Library, Inc., 1969), pp. 19–20.

16. Quoted in Stace, *op. cit.,* p. 338.

17. William Hordern, "A Theological Critique of the Psychedelic Experience," *Dialog,* Summer, 1964, p. 221.

18. *Ibid.,* p. 222.

19. Walter N. Pahnke and W. A. Richards, "Implications of LSD and Experimental Mysticism," *Journal of Religion and Health,* July, 1966, p. 194.

20. See Søren Kierkegaard, *Stages on Life's Way,* tr. by Walter Lowrie (Princeton University Press), 1940.

21. S. Cohen, *The Beyond Within,* p. 98.

22. H. A. Williams, "Theology and Self-awareness," in Alexander R. Vidler (ed.), *Soundings: Essays Concerning Christian Understanding* (London: Cambridge University Press, 1962), p. 72.

23. Robert C. Zaehner, *Mysticism: Sacred and Profane.*

24. Masters and Houston, *op. cit.,* p. 257.

25. See Hal Bridges' excellent chapter on "Psychology and Psychedelic Experience," *American Mysticism from William James to Zen.*

26. For an account of the debilitating effects of drugs on the hippie cult, see Donald B. Louria, *The Drug Scene,* and *Newsweek,* Aug. 18, 1969, p. 89.

27. Leary, *High Priest,* p. 158.

28. *Ibid.,* pp. 346–347.

29. Timothy Leary, *The Politics of Ecstasy* (G. P. Putnam's Sons, 1968), pp. 164–165.

Chapter 9. THE BIBLE AND DRUGS

1. John E. Kramer, "The Apothecary in the Bible and

Religious Lore," *American Journal of Pharmacy,* Nov., 1933, p. 554.

2. Cyril P. Bryan, *The Papyrus Ebers* (D. Appleton and Co., 1931), p. 15.

3. Arthur Rendle Short, *The Bible and Modern Medicine: A Survey of Health and Healing in the Old and New Testaments* (London: The Paternoster Press, 1953), p. 10.

4. See Francis Brown, S. R. Driver, and Charles Briggs, *A Hebrew and English Lexicon of the Old Testament* (Oxford: Clarendon Press, 1907), p. 955; and Kyle M. Yates, Jr., "The Theological Significance of Healing in the Old Testament" (unpublished doctoral dissertation, Southern Baptist Theological Seminary, 1955), p. 99.

5. See John Kramer, "The Drugs of the Bible," *American Journal of Pharmacy,* July, 1935, pp. 280–300; M. Zohary, "Flora," *The Interpreter's Dictionary of the Bible,* ed. by George A. Buttrick, *et al.,* 4 vols. (Abingdon Press, 1962), Vol. 2, pp. 284–302; R. H. Harrison, *Healing Herbs of the Bible* (Leiden: E. J. Brill, 1966); and Harold N. and A. L. E. Moldenke, *Plants of the Bible* (Chronica Botanica Company, 1952).

6. Kramer, *op. cit.,* p. 285.

7. See H. N. and A. L. E. Moldenke, *op. cit.,* p. 78.

8. Harrison, *op. cit.,* pp. 36–37.

9. A. G. Frazer, *Jacob and the Mandrakes* (London: Oxford University Press, 1917); reprinted from the British Academy, Vol. 8.

10. See Benjamin L. Gordon, *The Romance of Medicine* (F. A. Davis Company, 1949), pp. 372–374.

11. Harrison, *op. cit.,* p. 45.

12. Mark D. Altschule, "Editorial," *Medical Counterpoint,* July, 1970, p. 6. John Marco Allegro, lecturer in Old Testament and intertestamental studies at the University of Manchester, traces the origins of contemporary religions, including Judaism, Christianity, and Islam, to the fertility and mystery cults of the Near East, specifically among the worshipers of the "sacred mushroom," (*Amanita muscaria*) in *The Sacred Mushroom and the Cross* (Doubleday & Company, Inc., 1970).

God turns out to be a large red mushroom. So does the tree of good and evil. The New Testament, he claims, was written as an "underground handbook" for a fertility cult which ingested the hallucinogenic-producing mushroom. There is hardly a name, including that of Jesus, in the New Testament which does not have its origin in the mushroom-eating cult. Jesus was only a metaphor for the sacred mushroom. The man-child born of a virgin was actually the phallic-shaped mushroom which sprang up out of the ground without a visible seed (*ibid.*, p. 61).

Allegro claims to have made his discovery by comparing the connection between Biblical languages and the ancient Sumerian. In this way he was able to decipher the true meaning of the sacred names and incantations of the New Testament.

All of this sounds fantastic and it is. Allegro has an erotic hang-up. His efforts to derive his mushroom metaphors from the ancient Sumerian language are strained to the point of being ridiculous. An admitted agnostic, Allegro is bitter toward Christianity. This book is one of the ways in which he attempts to undermine and to discredit the Christian faith. No serious Biblical scholar accepts Allegro's views.

13. Raymond T. Stamm in *The Interpreter's Bible*, ed. by George A. Buttrick, 12 vols. (Abingdon Press, 1951–1957), Vol. 10, p. 562.

14. *Ibid.*

15. See A. E. Wilder-Smith, *The Drug Users: The Pharmacology of Turning On*, p. 143.

16. *Ibid.*, p. 144.

17. Leary, *The Politics of Ecstasy*, p. 302.

18. Wayne E. Oates, *The Holy Spirit in Five Worlds* (Association Press, 1968), pp. 26–38.

Chapter 10. THE CHURCH CONFRONTS THE DRUG CRISIS

1. "Toward the Critique of Hegel's Philosophy of Right," in Lewis S. Feuer (ed.), *Karl Marx and Friedrich Engels: Basic Writings on Politics and Philosophy* (Doubleday Anchor Book, 1959), p. 263.

2. Huston Smith, "Do Drugs Have a Religious Import?" in

David Solomon (ed.), *LSD the Consciousness-expanding Drug,*
p. 166.

3. See Paul L. Lehmann, *Ethics in a Christian Context*
(Harper & Row, Publishers, Inc., 1963), Ch. III.

4. *The Courier-Journal,* March 30, 1970, p. A-1.

5. *Ibid.,* June 9, 1970, p. A-1, and Aug. 9, 1970, p. A-22.

6. *Ibid.,* Feb. 23, 1970, p. A-7.

7. *Ibid.*

8. Howard J. Clinebell, Jr., *The Pastor and Drug Dependency,* p. 16.

9. "Pot and Parents," *Time,* Aug. 20, 1968, p. 45.

10. Norman Eddy, "The Church vs. Heroin," in Dan Wakefield (ed.), *The Addict,* p. 176.

BIBLIOGRAPHY

Abramson, Harold A. (ed.), *The Use of LSD in Psychotherapy and Alcoholism.* The Bobbs-Merrill Company, Inc., 1967.

Alpert, Richard, Cohen, Sidney, and Schiller, Lawrence, *LSD.* The New American Library of World Literature, Inc., 1966.

Ausubel, David P., *Drug Addiction: Physiological, Psychological, and Sociological Aspects.* Random House, Inc., 1958.

Bier, William C. (ed.), *Problems in Addiction: Alcoholism and Narcotics.* Fordham University Press, 1962.

Bloomquist, Edward R., *Marijuana.* Glencoe Press, 1969.

Blum, Richard H., *et al., Utopiates. The Use and Uses of LSD-25.* Atherton Press, 1964.

Braden, William, *The Private Sea: LSD and the Search for God.* Bantam Books, Inc., 1968.

Bridges, Hal, *American Mysticism from William James to Zen.* Harper & Row, Publishers, Inc., 1970.

Bulletin on Narcotics, July–September, 1956. United States Congress, Senate Committee on the Judiciary of the United States Senate, Findings and Recommendations of the Subcommittee on the Improvement in the Federal Criminal Code.

Carey, James T., *The College Drug Scene.* Prentice-Hall, Inc., 1968.

Casriel, Daniel H., *So Fair a House: The Story of Synanon.* Prentice-Hall, Inc., 1963.

Clark, Walter H., *Chemical Ecstasy: Psychedelic Drugs and Religion.* Sheed & Ward, Inc., 1969.

Clinebell, Howard J., Jr., *The Pastor and Drug Dependency*. Council Press, 1968.

Cohen, Sidney, *The Beyond Within: The LSD Story* (rev. ed.). Atheneum Publishers, 1964, 1967.

———— *The Drug Dilemma*. McGraw-Hill Book Company, Inc., 1969.

———— "Lysergic Acid Diethylamide: Side Effects and Complications," *Journal of Nervous and Mental Disease*, Jan., 1960.

Crockett, Richard W., *et al.* (eds.), *Hallucinogenic Drugs and Their Psychotherapeutic Use*. Charles C Thomas, Publishers, 1963.

Daedalus, "Toward the Year 2000," Summer, 1967.

DeBold, Richard C., and Leaf, Russell C. (eds.), *LSD, Man and Society*. Wesleyan University Press, 1968.

De Ropp, Robert S., *Drugs and the Mind*. Grove Press, Inc., 1960.

"Drug Therapy," Supplement to the *American Journal of Psychiatry*, Feb., 1968.

Duncan, Tommie L., *Understanding and Helping the Narcotic Addict*. Prentice-Hall, Inc., 1965.

Dunlap, Jane, *Exploring Inner Space*. Harcourt, Brace and World, Inc., 1961.

Ebin, David (ed.), *The Drug Experience*. Grove Press, Inc., 1965.

Facts Concerning the U. S. Public Service Hospital. Department of Health, Education, and Welfare, Washington, D.C., 1966.

Huxley, Aldous, *The Doors of Perception*. Harper & Row, Publishers, Inc., 1963.

James, William. *The Varieties of Religious Experience*. The New American Library of World Literature, Inc., 1952.

Leary, Timothy, *High Priest*. The World Publishing Company, 1968.

Leech, Kenneth, and Jordan, Brenda, *Drugs for Young People: Their Use and Misuse*. Wallington, Surrey, England: The Religious Education Press, Ltd., 1967.

Lindesmith, Alfred R., *The Addict and the Law*. Indiana University Press, 1965.

Lingeman, Richard R., *Drugs from A to Z: A Dictionary*. McGraw-Hill Book Company, Inc., 1969.

Louria, Donald B., *The Drug Scene*. McGraw-Hill Book Company, Inc., 1968.

Masters, R. E. L., and Houston, Jean, *The Varieties of Psychedelic Experience*. Holt, Rinehart and Winston, Inc., 1966.

Metzner, Ralph (ed.), *The Ecstatic Adventure*. The Macmillan Company, 1968.

Milbauer, Barbara, and Leinwand, Gerald, *Drugs*. Washington Square Press, 1970.

Narcotic and Drug Addiction, National Institute of Mental Health, Monograph No. 2, Public Health Service Publication, No. 1021. U.S. Government Printing Office, 1965.

Nowlis, Helen H., *Drugs on the College Campus*. Doubleday Anchor Book, 1969.

O'Donnell, John A., and Ball, John C. (eds.), *Narcotic Addiction*. Harper & Row Publishers, Inc., 1966.

Pahnke, Walter N., "Drugs and Mysticism: An Analysis of the Relationship Between Psychedelic Drugs and Mystical Consciousness." Unpublished doctoral dissertation, Harvard University, 1964. The full account of the Good Friday experiment is summarized by Pahnke and W. A. Richards in *Journal of Religion and Health*, July, 1966.

Psychedelic Information Center Bulletin. 26 Boylston Street, No. 3, Cambridge, Mass. 02138.

Schur, Edwin M., *Narcotic Addiction in Britain and America*. Indiana University Press, 1962.

Slotkin, James S., *The Peyote Religion*. Free Press, 1956.

Smith, David (ed.), *The New Social Drug*. Prentice-Hall, Inc., 1970.

Solomon, David (ed.), *LSD: The Consciousness-expanding Drug*. G. P. Putnam's Sons, 1964.

———— (ed.), *The Marijuana Papers*. The New American Library of World Literature, Inc., 1968.

Stace, Walter T., *Mysticism and Philosophy*. J. B. Lippincott Company, 1960.

Stafford, Peter G., and Golightly, Bonnie H., *LSD: The Problem-solving Psychedelic*. Award Books, 1967.

Task Force Report, *Narcotics and Drug Abuse*. U.S. Government Printing Office, 1967.

Journal of the American Medical Association. American Medical Association Division of Health Service, Department of Health Education, Chicago, Ill.

Unger, S. M., "Mescaline, LSD, Psilocybin, and Personality Change," *Psychiatry*, May, 1963.

Wakefield, Dan (ed.), *The Addict*. Fawcett Publications, Inc., 1968.

Wilder-Smith, A. E., *The Drug Users: The Psychopharmacology of Turning On*. Harold Shaw Publishers, 1969.

Winn, Mitchell (ed.), *Drug Abuse: Escape to Nowhere*. Smith, Kline and French Laboratories, 1967.

Zaehner, Robert C., *Mysticism: Sacred and Profane*. Oxford Galaxy Book, 1961. Among other things, an Oxford scholar, Zaehner, who has tried mescaline, holds that drugs do not induce truly religious mysticism.